CAREERS IN SPORT, FITNESS, AND EXERCISE

American Kinesiology Association

**Shirl J. Hoffman,
Project Coordinator**

Human Kinetics

Library of Congress Cataloging-in-Publication Data

Careers in sport, fitness, and exercise.
   p. cm.
  Includes index.
  ISBN-13: 978-0-7360-9566-2 (soft cover)
  ISBN-10: 0-7360-9566-7 (soft cover)
 1. Sports--Vocational guidance--United States. 2. Physical fitness--Vocational guidance--United
States. 3. Physical education and training--Vocational guidance--United States. I. American
Kinesiology Association.
  GV734.3.C39 2011
  796.023--dc22

                     2011010246
ISBN: 978-0-7360-9566-2

The web addresses cited in this text were current as of April 2011, unless otherwise noted.

Acquisitions Editor: Tom Heine; **Managing Editor:** Anne Cole; **Assistant Editor:** Elizabeth Evans;
Copyeditor: John Wentworth; **Indexer:** Nan Badgett; **Permissions Manager:** Dalene Reeder; **Graphic
Designer:** Joe Buck; **Graphic Artist:** Kim McFarland; **Cover Designer:** Keith Blomberg; **Photographer (cover):** © Human Kinetics; **Photo Production Manager:** Jason Allen; **Art Manager:** Kelly
Hendren; **Associate Art Manager:** Alan L. Wilborn; **Illustrations:** © Human Kinetics; **Printer:**
Seaway Printing

Human Kinetics books are available at special discounts for bulk purchase. Special editions or
book excerpts can also be created to specification. For details, contact the Special Sales Manager
at Human Kinetics.

Printed in the United States of America   20 19 18 17 16 15 14

The paper in this book is certified under a sustainable forestry program.

Human Kinetics
1607 N. Market Street
Champaign, IL 61820
USA

United States and International
Website: US.HumanKinetics.com
Email: info@hkusa.com
Phone: 1-800-747-4457

Canada
Website: Canada.HumanKinetics.com
Email: info@hkcanada.com

E5189

Tell us what you think!
Human Kinetics would love to hear what we
can do to improve the customer experience.
Use this QR code to take our brief survey.

CAREERS IN SPORT, FITNESS, AND EXERCISE

American Kinesiology Association

**Shirl J. Hoffman,
Project Coordinator**

Contents

Preface

This book, a joint effort of the American Kinesiology Association and Human Kinetics, is the first book of its kind. No other source presents detailed descriptions of the many options available to those seeking a career within the spheres of physical activity—namely exercise, sports, and fitness. The general information you can find on websites tends to be insufficient and superficial, lacking the depth and comprehensiveness we offer you here. In this book you will find for the first time anywhere the insights and advice of university professionals whose daily work involves preparing students for their careers. Bringing their enormous funds of knowledge about the exercise, sport, fitness, and physical activity industry to bear on the kinds of problems young people frequently encounter when exploring careers, these professionals have produced a resource invaluable not only for students and parents but for secondary school counselors and university advisors as well.

Kinesiology is the name that has emerged for the universe that houses the exciting worlds of physical activity. This term, kinesiology, has been adopted by many of the leading colleges and universities in North America, but some departments continue to use the terms *exercise and sport science, physical education,* or *health and human performance.* We are all talking about the same thing. The field of kinesiology—encompassing exercise, sports, fitness, and physical activity—is amazingly broad, offering an astonishing range of diverse careers in such areas as athletic training, sports medicine, director of community sport programs, personal fitness trainer, sport psychologist, physical education teacher, university researcher and teacher, fitness leader for geriatric centers, football coach, athletic director, and sports marketer—just to name a few. For students, parents, high school guidance counselors, and university academic advisors hoping to get firm footing in the exciting and flourishing cosmos of kinesiology, this book will be indispensable.

In chapters 1 and 2 we present a broad perspective of career development in the field, addressing the important questions students have when first beginning to explore their potential careers. In the rest of the book we provide the fundamentals, the essential information, on career opportunities available to those who graduate with a degree in kinesiology. Careers are grouped into separate but related categories. The many kinds of careers in the fitness industry are covered in chapter 3. Chapter 4 explores career opportunities in teaching, coaching, sport instruction, and sport psychology. In chapter 5 we discuss careers available for those who study sport management. Chapter 6 does the same for athletic training and sports medicine. Chapter 7 presents important insights for the increasing numbers of students enrolling in kinesiology programs who have set their postgraduate sights on careers in allied health fields such as physical therapy and medicine. Finally, in chapter 8, we discuss career possibilities for those considering the teaching of kinesiology at the college level or pursuing a career as a researcher.

Each chapter presents the skills and knowledge you will need to succeed in each career. You will also find helpful advice to increase your chances of success, an honest discussion of the benefits and drawbacks of each type of work, the physical and social settings in which you will probably work, a description of the type of co-workers with whom you will collaborate, the educational and certification requirements required to secure and maintain each career, and future economic prospects for the career. Advice from the writers is supplemented by helpful observations by professionals and clinicians working in the area, and from students preparing to do so.

To select a career that best matches your talents and interests you will want to do more than read this book. As the authors point out, career exploration must be a proactive process, a journey in which you take time to investigate many potential destinations. Think of this book as a map to help you explore the vast universe of kinesiology and to reach your destination. There are no shortcuts in this journey; your path to discovery requires a serious investment of time, energy, and thought. This book, together with your parents, friends, teachers, and advisors, can provide the crucial information you need to make the best choices, but in the end, it is up to *you* to choose your career path. A career is lifelong, stretching into years of self-discovery. We wish you luck and happiness on your journey.

Chapter 1

Examining the Big Picture

Shirl J. Hoffman, EdD

Choosing a career in the field of sport, exercise, and fitness is more complicated today than ever before. Never before have so many career options been available in so many exciting areas. Those interested in pursuing a career in sport can choose from coaching, sport marketing, sport promotion, athletic administration, sport officiating, athletic training, sport medicine, sport psychology, and sport law—and the list could go on. A career in the exercise and fitness industry can be very rewarding, but will it be a career as a personal trainer, exercise rehabilitation specialist, conditioning coach for athletes, fitness manager or owner of a gym or spa, exercise specialist for elderly populations, corporate fitness specialist, or in some other fitness specialty? You might have decided that a career in teaching sport and exercise or coaching is the best path for you, but will it be a career in teaching physical education (elementary, high school, or college), high-level sport instruction (golf pro, tennis pro, swimming pro, gymnastic instructor, etc.), exercise instruction at a fitness facility, or specialized instruction for those with disabilities?

Books, guidance counselors, parents, friends, coaches, teachers, Internet career sites . . . these all can be helpful to you in selecting your career. But ultimately the responsibility for making the decision is yours and yours alone. This being the case, you should take the decision process seriously by learning as much as you can about the careers that are out there. Career management begins before you even set foot on a college campus! There are specific steps to take. For example, talking to professors who teach in programs that prepare students for various careers can be a big help. Most professors will set aside time to talk to prospective students, but be sure to have your questions ready before showing up for the appointment. Talking to professionals working in a career area also can help you narrow your choices, but again, enter these discussions with well-thought-out questions about the career. When a professor or professional makes time to talk to you, they are doing you a favor, so act accordingly.

Serving as a volunteer in some aspect of the sport, exercise, and fitness industry is always a good idea; in fact, previous experience as a volunteer is mandatory for some careers. If you think you would like to be a high school basketball coach, ask a coach at a local school if you can help him or her on a volunteer basis; if you want to work as a fitness consultant, volunteer to work in a fitness facility. If you think a career in physical therapy is for you, volunteer at a local clinic. Because you lack the necessary training and education, it is unlikely that these experiences will involve you in the specific type of work you will do as a professional, but they will give experience in the work environment, help you establish a professional network, and buff up your résumé.

Before you do anything else, though, you should step back and look at all the career options available to you. Sometimes a clear sense of the big picture can help you make the best choice. In this book we provide that picture. The authors are experts who have their fingers on the pulse of developments in specific career areas; all of them work in higher education where they have years of experience preparing college students for careers in sport, exercise, and fitness. Most provide career counseling on a regular basis. Each of the chapters here offers in-depth information about the most popular career tracks in each career category, including information about what the job entails, where you will work, with whom you will work, the education and certifications you will need, and the future outlook for the career.

Locating a First-Rate Kinesiology Department to Prepare for Your Career

Often the key to a successful career is finding a college or university program that matches your interests and career aspirations. The **American Kinesiology Association (AKA)** is an association of over 100 college and university departments nationwide that prepare students for kinesiology careers. On its website, the **AKA** provides information regarding departments offering preparation in the career tracks discussed in this book. You can access this information at www.americankinesiology.org; click on the "Career Center" tab and then "Careers in Sport, Fitness, and Exercise." You will find instructions for identifying departments that sponsor curriculums matching your career interests.

THINKING BROADLY ABOUT CAREER CHOICES

In a perfect world everyone would find a career that is exciting, personally rewarding, challenging, and well paying. But this isn't a perfect world, which is probably
one reason why over five million people of ages 44 to 70 are currently embarking on "encore" (second or third) careers. Even though these midstream career
changes often turn out very well, they also can be disruptive to personal and
family life and set you back in your progress toward your ultimate career goals.
Thus, all things considered, it pays to choose your career path early and carefully,
taking into account your personal preferences and talents. You probably won't be
satisfied with a job simply because it pays well. If you are like most people you
want a job that is respected by the community, is performed under good working
conditions, provides reasonable time off for leisure pursuits, and offers reasonable
pay. Most people also prefer careers that contribute to the betterment of society,
require thinking and creativity, and allow them the freedom to make important
decisions about their work. Finding a career that meets all these requirements can
be a formidable challenge.

Careers and Jobs

Usually the term "career" connotes work that incorporates all or most of the characteristics listed previously. Unlike a "job," which usually is a simple matter of
working in return for money, a career
is a lifelong pursuit that requires
enormous personal investment and
prolonged training. Usually careers
reward workers with considerable
personal meaning—a sense that they
are making a valuable contribution
to the community or to society at
large. A job generally requires little
in the way of intellectual capacity or
creativity; most jobs are performed
under the supervision of someone
else. In many cases, jobs are part
time and the work they entail is
viewed by workers as tedious or bur-
densome. Someone lands a job as a
dishwasher at a restaurant, a cashier
at a movie theater, or as a newspaper
delivery person. By contrast, teachers, lawyers, physical therapists,
exercise rehabilitation specialists, or athletic directors pursue
careers as lifetime investments.

Laurence Gough – Fotolia

**Choosing a career requires careful thinking
and planning.**

Such positions involve a great deal of decision making, planning, advanced education, and a commitment to professional growth. They also require a certain amount of career management with an eye toward advancement.

Professions and Trades

Another category of work is known as the skilled trades—also called blue-collar work. Often these jobs pay workers on an hourly basis and offer few benefits. Electricians, machinists, plumbers, and heating and air conditioning workers are blue-collar workers, as are those who perform maintenance or assembly jobs. These jobs usually require technical training (either formal or informal) and might pay very well. According to the Bureau of Labor Statistics, the demand for such workers is likely to be great over the next many years. Usually those who work in a skilled trade see their work as a career, often shaping their entire lives around their expertise. Sometimes a skilled tradesman will refer to the "professional quality" of work they do, but most are not considered professionals as that term is understood in the workplace. By contrast, almost all the types of work described in this book are truly professions. Those who create their careers around them enjoy the advantages that professionals enjoy. They also take on the responsibilities of a professional.

What do we mean by professions and professionals? A *profession* is a distinctive type of work characterized by the following criteria:

➤ Centered on supplying services to a specific clientele
➤ Requires mastery of complex knowledge and skills
➤ Guided by formal and informal ethical codes intended to preserve the health and well-being of clients
➤ Prescribed certain expectations and standards that define acceptable conduct

Let's look briefly at a few of these characteristics as they apply to professionals—the group of individuals who are engaged in a particular profession:

➤ **Professionals master complex knowledge and skills.** One thing that sets professionals apart from laborers or blue-collar tradesmen is the level of knowledge required to perform their work. Anyone who has watched a plumber or computer repair technician recognizes that they usually possess a high level of technical knowledge and skill. But professionals are able to draw on a broader knowledge base anchored in research and theory. Professionals often describe their work as "translating theory into practice." Athletic trainers need to know more than how to tape an ankle or rehab a shoulder injury; they must have mastered a body of knowledge of anatomy, physiology, and applied biomechanics that allows them to put each situation they face in a very broad perspective. The skills that professionals possess are usually not manual skills but cognitive skills. Professionals make decisions based on their own professional judgments, and this requires a solid background of theoretical and factual knowledge that permits them to deduce the

Attending conferences offers opportunities for professionals to connect with others in their specific field and to rejuvenate their knowledge base.

correct steps that should be taken. The same is true for physical education teachers, athletic directors, exercise rehab specialists, and fitness programmers.

Most of the careers discussed in this book require, at a minimum, a baccalaureate degree offered in programs that prepare students to think in broad and complex ways and to solve important problems they will make as professionals. For most professionals, an undergraduate degree is not the end of their education—it is just the beginning. Professionals must keep current on the latest knowledge being developed in their field. One way they do this is through membership in professional associations or societies. These associations usually publish materials and hold regional and national conferences. For example, physical education teachers might be members of the American Alliance for Health, Physical Education, Recreation and Dance; exercise and conditioning specialists might belong to the American College of Sports Medicine or to the National Strength and Conditioning Association; and athletic trainers might be members of the National Athletic Trainers Association. Each career track described in this book has at least one relevant professional association that serves its members by offering updated information about professional practice. If you are committed to becoming a professional you must also be committed to learning, not merely in college but throughout your career. True professionals are by nature curious. They want to know about the latest developments in their fields and how they can improve their skills and knowledge.

➤ **Professionals perform services for clients.** Tradesmen have customers; professionals serve clients, patients, or students. Providing service to specific populations, ideally in the spirit of helpfulness and concern, is the lifeblood of the professions. Although (unfortunately) not all professionals are as service oriented as they should be, most who work in the sport, exercise, and fitness arena are committed to their clients. Possessing a strong desire to help people is a fundamental requirement for anyone entering the professions, but being a successful professional requires more than wanting to give a helping hand. A spirit of helpfulness unaccompanied by a level of competence that enables you to render actual assistance isn't likely to keep you employed. A golf pro who wants to help but is unable to detect the flaw in a student's swing, a physical education teacher who lacks the skill to adapt a lesson to a class's needs, or a rehabilitation exercise specialist unable to motivate an elderly resident of a nursing home to exercise can't render services to their clients despite their keen desire to do so.

➤ **Professionals adhere to established ethical codes.** Usually clients have faith in professionals to act in their best interests. Professionals who violate this trust by placing their own interests ahead of the client's interests are not only a disservice to their profession but risk being sanctioned by their colleagues. Usually professional associations publish ethical standards and codes of conduct that outline acceptable professional behavior. Figure 1.1 lists some of the ethical principles published by the Association of Applied Sport Psychology (AASP) intended to ensure that sport psychologists act in the best interests of their clients.

If you are committed to pursuing a career as a professional you must also be committed to serving. This means your career objectives should extend far beyond the goal of bettering yourself financially or advancing your status in the workplace. Good professionals also set their sights on making solid and lasting contributions to the betterment of society, and they do this through selfless serving of their clientele.

➤ **Professionals adhere to standards of their own subculture.** Although professionals work in a variety of contexts, general professional standards apply no matter the locale in which they work. Politeness and respect toward those they are serving are essential. Professionals tend to be well organized. They do not (usually) work on an hourly basis, but they don't hesitate to work extra hours when a task requires it. They often work weekends. They dress according to accepted occupational standards and are attentive to matters of personal hygiene and grooming. A sport program director that comes to a board meeting in sweaty clothes more appropriate for a workout, a cardiac rehabilitation specialist who is always late for her sessions, or a personal trainer with bad hygiene are not conducting themselves in a professional manner. Of course these general expectations apply to professionals in any field, but each profession usually has a set of specific expectations used to judge the appropriateness of the professional's conduct. For example, fitness leaders and physical education teachers might be expected to model the physically active life, to refrain from smoking, and to maintain a level of fitness appropriate for their age.

The sooner you become socialized into your chosen profession and learn the expectations of the work culture, the more valuable you will be to prospective

Ethical Principles and Standards for Members of the Association of Applied Sport Psychology

Sport psychologists who work with athletes and who are members of the Association of Applied Sport Psychology (AASP) are expected to adhere to a strict code of professional ethics. The association has published an ethics code for its members that covers a multitude of issues. The code has as its centerpiece five general principles that can be summarized as follows:

- **Competence:** Members of AASP should keep abreast of their field and recognize the limitations of their knowledge and skills. They are committed to protecting the welfare of all whom they serve.
- **Integrity:** Members of the AASP are honest and fair in reporting their qualifications, services, products, and fees and avoid improper dual relationships.
- **Respect for people's rights and dignity:** Members of AASP respect the rights of those with whom they work to confidentiality, self-determination, and autonomy
- **Concern for others' welfare:** Members of AASP work to resolve conflicts that arise with colleagues, and they do not exploit or mislead others.
- **Social responsibility:** AASP members are aware of their responsibility to the community; they make their work public so as to benefit others and strive to prevent misuse of their work.

Figure 1.1 Professional associations use standards to define acceptable professional behavior.

Reprinted, by permission, from American Association of Sport Physiology.
Available: http://appliedsportpsych.org/resource-center/professionals

employers when seeking a position. For this reason, growing numbers of students in college professional preparatory programs seek opportunities to immerse themselves in the professional subculture of their anticipated careers by volunteering to work in clinics, schools, and community agencies while still enrolled in college. Although usually not counted as course work, such extracurricular activities provide experiences to give you a head start when the time comes for applying for career positions after graduation.

TACKLING A TOUGH DECISION

Some people know from an early age what career they want to follow. They might have been influenced by parents or friends or by a professional while still in high school. Many young people choose to become coaches because of the influence of their high school coach. A young athlete who has suffered an injury and been rehabilitated through the services of an athletic trainer or physical therapist might make the decision to help rehabilitate others who have been injured in sports. But for many people selecting a career is an agonizing task. Difficulty in making the tough decision can be a crippling barrier to getting an early start on their career. Uncertainty about what do with their lives plagues some young people long after they have enrolled in college.

Why is making a career decision so difficult for some people? Interestingly, the topic has been extensively researched by those working in the area of counseling psychology—an indication of just how prevalent career indecisiveness is among young people. It appears that many factors can be a hindrance in deciding on a career. Lack of motivation, for example, not only causes some people to postpone making a decision but often prevents them from rationally investigating career possibilities. Some college students refer to the prospect of selecting a career as entering the "great black hole."

Failure to have access to adequate information can also be a barrier to making a career decision. This might include lack of information about your own capabilities and interests. In such cases a young person might not know the answer to two very important questions: *What am I able to do?* and *What do I want to do?* The first question regards capabilities. What special interests and talents do you possess that might be exploited in the workplace? Answers to this question usually require the services of a career counselor who, through skillful questioning, testing, and analysis of your responses on occupational aptitude tests can help you narrow the general category of work that best matches your abilities. Many of these tests are based on psychologist John Holland's research, which has identified six vocational personalities and work environments: realistic, investigative, artistic, social, enterprising, and conventional. Hypothetically, each personality type lends itself to specific career clusters (figure 1.2). Other self-administered career aptitude tests are easily found on the Internet—you might check out Career Explorer, Job Diagnosis, and Career Colleges, to name a few. See the Resources at the end of this book for details.

You might find that answering the second question (What do I want to do?) is much easier if you have first answered What am I able to do? Ideally, talking with a career counselor or accessing online career aptitude tests will lead you to a professional career that you do not simply like, but one that you like passionately. But even with test results showing which category of work best suits your abilities and interests, making the final decision still can be challenging. Taking the time to answer the questions in figure 1.3 might be a big help in the process. Those who have engaged in such a rational, systematic career search are least likely to be plagued by career indecision. Yet in the end, you and you alone must make your choice. Putting off the decision is deciding not to decide!

PREPARING FOR YOUR CAREER

Having identified a career, your next step is to seek out the best preparation for it. Again, the advantage goes to those who have already begun to think about a career before they graduate from high school. Selecting high school courses that

Holland's Personality Types and Careers in Kinesiology*

• **Realistic personality:** Values practical and mechanical experiences such as operating machines, growing crops, or raising animals. Does not enjoy social interaction and would not likely enjoy teaching. Possible career choices include police work, firefighting, and electrician or carpentry work. Career opportunities are limited for this personality type in the field of kinesiology.

• **Investigative personality:** Possesses superior skills at analyzing and understanding science and math problems. They tend not to be leaders or salespersons; they are more comfortable in laboratory environments. Those who pursue careers as researchers in exercise physiology, biomechanics of sport, sport sociology, or other topics in kinesiology might have investigative personalities.

• **Artistic personality:** Enjoys creative activities such as art, drama, crafts, dance, music, or creative writing; generally avoids highly ordered or repetitive activities. Artistic personalities are best suited to work as writers, actors, artists, musicians, or dancers.

• **Social personality:** Enjoys helping people; values friendliness and trustworthiness in others. This personality tends to excel in careers such as nursing, counseling, dental hygiene, physical therapy, and medicine. Social students often pursue careers in athletic training and sport medicine.

• **Enterprising personality:** Tends to be ambitious, energetic, sociable. People with this personality are self-starters who enjoy positions of leadership. They are less interested in analyzing or conducting scientific observations than in getting something practical accomplished. Often they pursue careers in business or politics. Managers of fitness facilities, coaches, and school principals are likely to have enterprising personalities.

• **Conventional personality:** Enjoys working with machines, numbers, facts, and records. They prefer highly structured, orderly work that follows a set plan. Conventional personality types are often bookkeepers, bank tellers, or clerks. Most careers in kinesiology are not readily compatible with this personality type.

*These personality types are not mutually exclusive. Two or more types can be found in the same individual.

Figure 1.2 Your personality type matters when selecting a career.

provide you with the basic knowledge you need for beginning a college program in kinesiology is essential. Most (but not all) careers connected with kinesiology deal with the moving body. Thus coursework that emphasizes biology, chemistry, physiology, and psychology helps provide this foundation. On the other hand, if you envision a career in sport management, extra coursework in business or management is helpful. If your career plans are to study kinesiology as preparatory

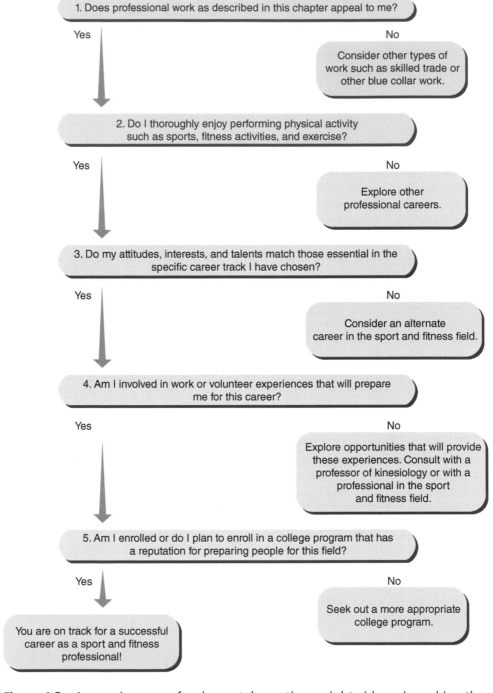

Decisions for Career Tracks in Sport and Fitness

1. Does professional work as described in this chapter appeal to me?

Yes

No
Consider other types of work such as skilled trade or other blue collar work.

2. Do I thoroughly enjoy performing physical activity such as sports, fitness activities, and exercise?

Yes

No
Explore other professional careers.

3. Do my attitudes, interests, and talents match those essential in the specific career track I have chosen?

Yes

No
Consider an alternate career in the sport and fitness field.

4. Am I involved in work or volunteer experiences that will prepare me for this career?

Yes

No
Explore opportunities that will provide these experiences. Consult with a professor of kinesiology or with a professional in the sport and fitness field.

5. Am I enrolled or do I plan to enroll in a college program that has a reputation for preparing people for this field?

Yes

No
Seek out a more appropriate college program.

You are on track for a successful career as a sport and fitness professional!

Figure 1.3 Answering some fundamental questions might aid you in making the right career choice.

Adapted, by permission, from S. Hoffman, 2009, *Introduction to kinesiology online study guide,* 3rd ed. (Champaign, IL: Human Kinetics).

for a graduate program in physical therapy, medicine, or athletic training, you should secure opportunities to volunteer at clinical sites. Investing time in these experiences, investigating the GPA requirements for admission to undergraduate and graduate programs in a specialized academic program, and conversations with your guidance counselors will help you determine the likelihood that you will be able to meet the academic challenges for the program you want to pursue.

As we have mentioned, the route to any professional career begins at a college or university that offers rigorous and timely educational programs. Fortunately, there are well over 800 programs in North America that prepare people for the sport, exercise, and fitness industry. As the demand for workers in the industry has increased so has student enrollment in programs that prepare these workers. Over the past five years, student enrollment in many college and university kinesiology departments has grown enormously, in some cases exceeding a 50 percent increase. Selecting a college that is right for you is very important, but selecting a department that matches your interests and career plans is important as well. A university ranked high by *U.S. News and World Report,* for example, doesn't tell you much about the quality of the sport, exercise, and fitness program offered by that institution. If you envision a career in sport management or athletic training, and the college you were planning to attend offers only a few courses and no specialized programs in these areas, it is best to consider other institutions.

If your career search has led you to explore the websites of many college and university departments, you might have difficulty locating the precise department that prepares students for careers in sport, exercise, and fitness. In some colleges the department might be called "health, physical education, and recreation;" in others it might be known as "sport science" or "sport studies," and at still other institutions it may be called "exercise science," "health and human performance," or "kinesiology." This confusion stems in part from the peculiarities in organizational structures across colleges and universities. For example, at most larger universities, separate departments offer separate degree programs in health or recreation, but in smaller institutions these programs are often included in a single department. In these cases you are likely to come across a "health, human performance, and recreation" department.

This diversity in department names reflects the enormous expansion of our evolving field. Fifty years ago what was a field largely limited to preparing physical education teachers and coaches has expanded exponentially and now serves as the training ground for multiple careers. The name used by most of the forward-looking departments in the country is *kinesiology,* which is the science of movement or physical activity. The American Kinesiology Association (AKA), a national organization of college and university departments, defines kinesiology as

> "an academic discipline which involves the study of physical activity and its impact on health, society, and quality of life. It includes, but is not limited to, such areas of study as exercise science, sports management, athletic training and sports medicine, socio-cultural analyses of sports, sport and exercise

psychology, fitness leadership, physical education-teacher education, and pre-professional training for physical therapy, occupational therapy, medicine and other health related fields."

Owing to the influence of organizations such as National Academy of Kinesiology, the American Academy of Kinesiology and Physical Education, and the National Association for Kinesiology and Physical Education in Higher Education, as well as its adoption by most of the leading departments in the country, the term *kinesiology* is rapidly becoming the label of choice for the field. So, keep in mind that when we refer to kinesiology in this book we are talking about the same field of study denoted by other names as well.

IDENTIFYING A HIGH-QUALITY KINESIOLOGY PROGRAM

Departments of kinesiology should be judged first and foremost on the quality of the programs they offer. Most departments require students to take a cluster of departmental courses known as "the core." This core requirement is important because it forms the groundwork for more specialized knowledge taught in various concentrations (e.g., teacher education, athletic training, etc.). The very best programs provide a solid grounding in the broad field of kinesiology, including exercise physiology; biomechanics; motor development, control and learning; sport psychology; and sociocultural analysis of sport and physical activity. See the American Kinesiology Association's (AKA) recommendations listed in figure 1.4. The specifics of this core varies substantially from department to department; sometimes, for example, courses and subject areas are combined into single courses.

High-quality programs require internship experiences of varying durations; offer opportunities for students to get involved in research under the direction of faculty mentors; present opportunities to gain leadership experience in campus organizations; and facilitate students' efforts to volunteer in campus or community service projects. For many exercise science classes, you also want to ensure that laboratory experiences are part of the instructional program. Here are some hints for selecting a department that will meet your personal and professional needs:

➤ **Select a college or university that suits your general tastes.** Are you afraid of getting lost in the shuffle of a large state university? If so, there are scores of smaller liberal arts institutions that offer programs in kinesiology. Although these schools do not have high-profile intercollegiate sport programs, which many students find attractive, they usually offer small classes and opportunities to establish close relationships with faculty. If, on the other hand, you think you would be happiest in a larger school, limit your search to those institutions.

➤ **Examine the academic catalog.** Is ample coursework offered in the kinesiology department to support your study? Does the program offer a concentration or a full-fledged degree program in kinesiology?

Recommended Core Areas for Coursework in a Kinesiology Curriculum

- Physical activity in health, wellness, and quality of life
- Scientific foundations of physical activity
- Cultural, historical, and philosophical dimensions of physical activity
- The practice of physical activity

Figure 1.4 The AKA recommends that all college and university undergraduate degree programs in kinesiology offer coursework and experiences in these general core categories. See sample core on page 23.

Reprinted from American Kinesiology Association 2003.

➤ **Review the departmental website.** Does the department seem alive? Are exciting things going on?

➤ **Examine the faculty directory of the department on the website.** Review their credentials, if listed on the site. Do faculty members share your interests? Are they fully engaged in their profession? Are they active in academic or professional societies? Are they sponsoring interesting projects? Are they publishing in academic and professional journals?

➤ **Plan to visit the department.** Set up an appointment with the department head or with faculty members working in areas that interest you. Send them an e-mail to introduce yourself before you meet with them.

➤ **Talk to students during your visit.** Current students offer a unique perspective on the department that others cannot. Use caution, though—do not accept opinions blindly; if students have had bad experiences with a single professor this might have tainted their feelings about the entire department. Talk to as many students as possible to get a complete picture.

Some careers covered in this book require only a bachelor's degree; others require a master's or doctoral level education. Some career tracks such as medicine and physical therapy require advanced training that goes well beyond the undergraduate degree in kinesiology. Increasing numbers of students enrolled in kinesiology programs are planning a career in one of these advanced specializations. They appreciate how scientific coursework required in kinesiology provides a foundation for further study in their chosen health-related careers. Other career tracks such as sports medicine and athletic training might call for a master's degree, and certification to teach in some states requires a master's degree as well. Thus, your undergraduate degree might be only a starting point leading you into your career in sport, exercise, fitness, and kinesiology. We wish you the best as you embark on a career in the exciting area of sport, exercise and fitness!

Chapter 2

Making Intelligent Career Choices in Kinesiology

Wojtek Chodzko-Zajko, PhD

As head of the department of kinesiology and community health at the University of Illinois at Urbana-Champaign (one of the oldest and arguably most venerable kinesiology programs in the nation), perhaps the most frequent question posed to me by prospective students and their parents is this: What will my son or daughter be able to do with a degree in kinesiology? In my response I try to explain that in some departments in the university it *is* possible to make fairly specific predictions about what a graduate from an academic program will do upon leaving the university. For example, the majority of students from the department of speech and hearing sciences eventually assume positions as speech pathologists or clinical audiologists, and this has always been the primary career path for students enrolled in that department. However, not all departments and academic programs are able to make statements about career choices for their graduates with such specificity. For example, undergraduate students in philosophy, history, mathematics, romance languages, and a host of other departments often have no precise idea about what they will do when they graduate from college. I want to quickly add that this does not mean there is anything wrong with history, philosophy, math, romance languages, or any of the many other departments not linked to particular career paths or professions. There will always be room in universities for students seeking a broad based liberal education, and most students from these disciplines go on to fulfilling careers and have important roles in society. I go on to explain to the anxious parent that kinesiology as a field falls somewhere between speech and hearing science and philosophy on the career prediction ladder. Most of our graduates move on to jobs and careers linked in some way to physical activity, sport, or human movement, but precisely what they do is up to them and varies considerably from student to student. I add that this broad and growing diversity of career choices is a good thing that provides students with a wide variety of options with respect to how they will be able to link their love of physical activity, sports, and human movement to an interesting and rewarding future career.

EMERGENCE OF A SCIENCE OF KINESIOLOGY

My conversation with my student's parent would have sounded quite different 50 or 60 years ago. In the 1950s and '60s, career paths of our undergraduate students were much more predictable. At that time our department was known as the department of physical education, for good reason, because more than half of our graduating seniors went on to careers as physical education teachers. In those days it was quite easy to predict our students' career goals. The majority became PE teachers or coaches with only a small percentage going on to alternative careers in other health and physical activity–related fields. Today, only about five percent of the more than 1,200 undergraduate students in the kinesiology and community health department at Illinois are preparing for careers as physical education teachers or coaches. Although the change in emphasis from physical education toward a more diverse set of physical activity and sport-related careers has differed in extent from university to university, there can be little doubt that a gradual shift has occurred in career choices for our majors. Why has this shift occurred?

In the 1970s, at universities in the United States and beyond, scholars began to re-examine the intellectual and philosophical roots of physical education, its curriculum, and how it was taught. As a result of this debate, two major outcomes emerged that would change the face of physical education in the university setting forever. First was the decision to initiate a process to change the name of our field from physical education to the more encompassing label of kinesiology. At that time, kinesiology was broadly envisioned to be the study of the art and science of human movement. Today the definition has evolved somewhat: The American Kinesiology Association defines the field of kinesiology as " . . . an academic discipline which involves the study of physical activity and its impact on health, society, and quality of life. It includes, but is not limited to, such areas of study as exercise science, sports management, athletic training and sports medicine, socio-cultural analyses of sports, sport and exercise psychology, fitness leadership, physical education-teacher education, and preprofessional training for physical therapy, occupational therapy, medicine and other health related fields." Although not all universities' physical education departments ultimately changed their names to kinesiology, many did, and kinesiology is now one of the most frequently used term to describe departments formerly known as physical education.

The second major outcome of the movement that led to the re-examination of role and function of physical education departments in the university was a decision to reform the curriculum in order to educate students in the core disciplinary areas of the new field of kinesiology. Undergraduate students around the country began, in much greater numbers than ever before, to study core disciplinary areas of kinesiology, including exercise physiology, biomechanics, motor control and motor development, exercise and sport psychology, sociology of sport, and sport history. An extremely important outcome of this period of curricular reform was an increased level of preparation of our students in the body of knowledge related to physical activity, which permitted them to consider a broader range of careers than previously possible.

UNPRECEDENTED OPPORTUNITIES AND DAUNTING CHALLENGES FOR FUTURE KINESIOLOGISTS

As departments have incorporated a deeper and broader study of the scientific basis of the relation between physical activity, sport, and health, this has led to an explosion in career choices for our graduates in kinesiology. While the expansion of knowledge about the benefits of physically active lifestyles has led to an increased market demand for individuals with a background in kinesiology, it has also caused a significant increase in the amount and diversity of knowledge, skills, and abilities graduates of kinesiology programs will be expected to acquire. Increasingly, graduates are asked to function in an interdisciplinary environment that emphasizes a multifaceted approach to health, sport, and wellness. This new interdisciplinary approach to kinesiology provides both opportunities and challenges for our future graduates.

The Emergence of a Rigorous Evidence-Based Science

We are living at a time in which there is a growing appreciation for the importance of regular physical activity as an integral component of a healthy lifestyle. Over the past 20 to 30 years a substantial body of evidence has accumulated regarding the benefits that accrue to people of all ages who participate in regular physical activity. In 2008, for example, the Department of Health and Human Services (DHHS) published, for the first time, official U.S. Government Physical Activity Guidelines. The authors of these guidelines conclude that there is strong evidence that men, women, and children who are more active are healthier and enjoy substantially better quality of life compared to less active people. The World Health Organization (WHO) has suggested the benefits of physical activity fall into two basic categories (summarized in table 2.1):

1. Benefits of physical activity for individuals
2. Societal benefits of promoting physically active lifestyles

Table 2.1 Benefits of Physical Activity

Individual benefits		
Physiological	**Psychological**	**Social**
Immediate benefits · **Glucose levels:** Physical activity helps regulate blood glucose levels. · **Catecholamine activity:** Both adrenalin and noradrenalin levels are stimulated by physical activity. · **Improved sleep:** Physical activity has been shown to enhance sleep quality and quantity.	· **Relaxation:** Appropriate physical activity enhances relaxation. · **Reduces stress and anxiety:** There is evidence that regular physical activity can reduce stress and anxiety. · **Enhanced mood state:** Numerous people report elevations in mood state following appropriate physical activity.	· **Empowering older individuals:** Sedentary lifestyles threaten to reduce independence and self-sufficiency. Appropriate physical activity can empower individuals and assist them in playing a more active role in society. · **Enhanced social and cultural integration:** Physical activity programs, particularly in small groups or in social environments, enhance social and intercultural interactions.
Long-term effects · **Aerobic and cardiovascular endurance:** Substantial improvements in almost all aspects of cardiovascular functioning have been observed following appropriate physical training. · **Resistive training and muscle strengthening:** Individuals of all ages can benefit from muscle strengthening exercises. Resistance training can have a significant impact on the maintenance of independence and functioning. · **Flexibility:** Exercise which stimulates movement throughout the range of motion assists in the preservation and restoration of flexibility. · **Balance/coordination:** Regular activity helps prevent and/or postpone the age-associated declines in balance and coordination that are a major risk factor for falls. · **Velocity of movement:** Behavioral slowing is a characteristic of advancing age. Individuals who are regularly active can often postpone these age-related declines.	· **General well being:** Improvements in almost all aspects of psychological functioning have been observed following periods of extended physical activity. · **Improved mental health:** Regular exercise can make an important contribution in the treatment of several mental illnesses, including depression and anxiety neuroses. · **Cognitive improvements:** Regular physical activity may help postpone age-related declines in central nervous system processing speed and improve reaction time. · **Motor control and performance:** Regular activity helps prevent and/or postpone the age-associated declines in both fine and gross motor performance. · **Skill acquisition:** New skills can be learned and existing skills refined by all individuals regardless of age.	· **Enhanced integration:** Regularly active individuals are less likely to withdraw from society and more likely to actively contribute to the social milieu. · **Formation of new friendships:** Participation in physical activity, particularly in small groups and other social environments stimulates new friendships and acquaintances. · **Widened social and cultural networks:** Physical activity frequently provides individuals with an opportunity to widen available social networks. · **Role maintenance and new role acquisition:** A physically active lifestyle helps foster the stimulating environments necessary for maintaining an active role in society, as well as for acquiring positive new roles. · **Enhanced intergenerational activity:** In many societies, physical activity is a shared activity which provides opportunities for intergenerational contact.

Societal benefits of promoting physical activity

· **Reduced health and social care costs:** Physical inactivity and sedentary living contributes to decreased independence and the onset of many chronic diseases. Physically active lifestyles can help postpone the onset of inactivity related disorders and conditions, thereby significantly reducing health and social care costs.

· **Enhancing productivity:** Physically active lifestyles help people maintain functional independence and optimize their ability to actively participate in society.

· **Promoting a positive and active image:** A society that promotes physically active lifestyles for people of all ages (especially older persons) is more likely to reap the benefits of older individuals' experience and wisdom. Many older adults voluntarily adopt a sedentary lifestyle, which eventually threatens to reduce independence and self-sufficiency.

Information gathered from the U.S. Bureau of Labor Statistics website: http://www.bls.gov/oco/ocos251.htm#training. Bureau of Labor Statistics, 2008.

The WHO recommends that virtually all individuals should participate in physical activity on a regular basis and that society has a responsibility to advocate for broad-based participation in physical activity whenever possible. Over the past 20 years or so there has been a widespread adoption of physical activity recommendations, and physical activity interventions are increasingly recommended as an essential component in the prevention, treatment, and management of noncommunicative diseases and conditions.

These advances in our understanding of the scientific basis of the relation between physical activity participation and health have had important consequences for students in the field of kinesiology. In addition to serving in important traditional roles as teachers and coaches, athletic trainers, sport administrators, and so on, graduates of kinesiology departments are making a difference in physical activity–related positions in hospitals, clinics, corporations, public health departments, and a wide variety of other public and private sector professions. For many of our students, the increased recognition of the importance of physical activity as a preventive and therapeutic medicine has led to a substantial increase in employment opportunities in the health- and sport-related professions.

Physical Activity Promotion as a New Public Health Focus

One example of a profession that has become more accessible to kinesiology graduates is public health. Public health is the discipline charged with preventing disease, prolonging life, and promoting health and well-being through the organized efforts and informed choices of society, organizations, communities, and individuals. Until fairly recently public health was concerned primarily with issues related to sanitation, vaccination, and the control of infectious diseases. But recent years have seen an increased awareness of a new role for public health in the prevention and management of the chronic diseases and conditions that emerge as a result of unhealthy lifestyle behaviors. Increasingly, public health departments are charged with implementing evidence-based physical activity and healthy-eating programs in an attempt to stem the widespread epidemic of obesity and inactivity-related disorders. Recognizing the need to align with this important new focus within public health, many kinesiology programs in North American universities and beyond have begun to establish master of public health (MPH) programs, either on their own or in partnership with other academic units across the university. These programs have the potential to be effective in the battle against lifestyle-related diseases.

The WHO has proposed a model of public health (figure 2.1) practice built on three pillars of public health that are highly interrelated and mutually dependent:

1. Building **awareness** of the importance of living active and healthy lives
2. Improving the **assessment** of individual, environmental, and societal risk factors for developing chronic diseases
3. Facilitating the design and implementation of **interventions** to help prevent, manage, or treat inactivity-related problems

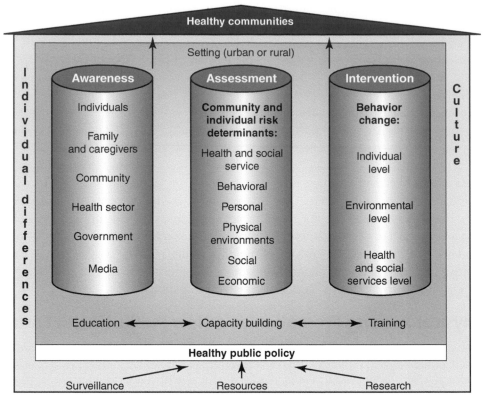

Figure 2.1 WHO health communities model of public health practice.

Kinesiologists can play a critical role in each of these areas, helping to build awareness of the importance of active and healthy lifestyles, assisting in identifying risk factors and predictors of inactivity-related conditions, and recommending and implementing state-of-the-art interventions for the prevention, management, and treatment of lifestyle-related disorders.

Redefining Healthy Lifestyles

A logical extension of the WHO model of public health has been a move away from the promotion of physical activity programs that target individuals to a much broader health promotion strategy focused on changing whole communities. For example, the WHO launched a worldwide initiative to support the development of healthy cities. The goal of the WHO Healthy City initiative is to encourage communities around the world to take action to make the environment more supportive and accommodating to people of all ages. The WHO report suggests that making cities healthier is one of the most effective policy approaches for responding to chronic diseases and conditions. A healthy city is one in which policies, services, and structures are designed to enable residents to live actively, be secure, enjoy good health, and participate fully in society.

Star Student: James

In high school, James enjoyed participating in sports and physical activity but was not quite good enough to make the varsity teams. He was interested in biology and science and was a strong student with grades in the top 10 percent of his graduating class. After consulting with his high school academic advisor, James decided to apply for admission to an undergraduate kinesiology program with a goal of progressing to graduate school in physical therapy. He believed that a kinesiology major was ideal for combining his interest in sport and physical activity with his strengths in biology and science. While completing his undergraduate degree, James participated in several internships and practicum experiences, including an internship at the local hospital cardiac rehabilitation program and another at a retirement community. After graduating with his undergrad degree, James accepted a position working for a large corporation in their wellness center but is considering going to grad school in a few years to continue his education.

James, Bachelor of Science in Kinesiology Graduate

Healthy cities benefit everyone. Improving air and water quality protects growing children and older people who are sensitive to environmental exposure. Secure neighborhoods are safer for children, youth, women, and older adults. Barrier-free buildings and streets enhance the mobility and independence of both younger and older persons with disabilities. One important characteristic of healthy cities is a commitment to accessible and affordable parks and recreation systems that provide opportunities for citizens to play games and sports. Many kinesiology graduates will have opportunities to work in park districts and sport centers as coaches, exercise leaders, wellness consultants, and personal trainers. Increasingly physical education teachers are becoming involved in healthy city movements, supplementing their traditional roles teaching physical education classes with organizing after-school physical activity and sport programs.

Creating a healthier society in the 21st century will not be easy. Healthy communities will be those that find a way to simultaneously involve and engage many different groups including experts in health and social services, education, employment and labor, finance, social security, housing, transportation, and both rural and urban development. Kinesiologists will play an important role in the partnerships needed to build healthier communities. For example, some kinesiology students will become PE teachers who introduce children to sport and movement skills. Others will be physical activity and fitness specialists working in leisure and sport centers, prescribing physical activity and leading exercise programs. Still others will become athletic trainers and physical therapists helping people with the treatment and rehabilitation of sport-related injuries. Many kinesiology students will work in professional sports, in the media, and on medical and legal aspects of sport. Regardless of which career direction their education takes them, kinesiology graduates will have important functions in building healthy and active communities around the world.

STRATEGIES FOR SUCCESS AS A KINESIOLOGY STUDENT

As you will discover as you read on, an astonishing diversity of career options are now available to graduates of kinesiology programs (figure 2.2). Kinesiology graduates are working in a huge variety of different professions, most of which have in

Athletic trainer	Exercise physiology
Occupational therapy	Sport journalism
Physical therapy	Sport law
Physician	Rehabilitation counselor
Physician's assistant	Optometrist
Chiropractor	Dentist
Cardiac rehabilitation	Corporate health
Corporate fitness	Chiropractor
Personal training	Health educator
Research scientist	Health law
Physical education/teaching	Health promotion
Coach	Health planning
Athletic director	Health consulting
Athletic administration	Health administration
Rehabilitation	Health marketing

Figure 2.2 Common career choices for kinesiology students.

common an association to physical activity, sport, and human health. Given the large number of career options, you might wonder how to navigate through them to identify a career choice that works for you. Let's look at strategies for success I discuss with my freshmen students in the Introduction to Kinesiology course they take in their first semester as undergraduates.

Build a Sound Foundation

Most university programs identify a series of core kinesiology courses taken by all majors regardless of their career intentions. A typical kinesiology core curriculum consists of a group of undergraduate courses in exercise physiology, motor behavior, biomechanics, sport and society, and exercise psychology usually taken in the first two years of the program (figure 2.3). Wise students delay making long-term decisions in regard to what kind of kinesiologist they want to be until they have sampled all their program has to offer by taking all or most of the core courses.

Introduction to Public Health

Physical Activity and Health

Introduction to Kinesiology

Analysis of Basic Movement

Social Science of Human Movement

Bioscience of Human Movement

Social and Psychological Aspects of Physical Activity

Bioenergetics of Movement

Biomechanics of Human Movement

Coordination, Control, and Skill

Motor Develop, Growth, and Form

Figure 2.3   Typical core courses for undergraduate kinesiology students.

Students' experiences in these foundation classes often serve to turn them on to a particular aspect of kinesiology that they subsequently explore further in elective courses taken in their junior and senior years. I firmly believe one of the best moves future kinesiologists can make is getting a sound background in the fundamentals of the discipline. Successful careers are built on sound foundations.

Make Internships, Practicums, and Summer Jobs Work for You

Most kinesiology programs give undergraduate students several opportunities to participate in on-the-job training through a variety of formal, supervised internship experiences. Students typically gain career-related experience by participating in internships in hospitals, public health departments, corporate wellness programs, youth sport programs, summer camps, sport centers, retirement communities, and other work sites as part of a variety of internships and team-based learning experiences. The wise student supplements these formal internships with summer jobs and other paid or unpaid employment that provides them with additional work experience in areas related to physical activity and sport. Many students must work part time or full time while making their way through college, and students able to find jobs that broaden their background and experience are more likely to succeed in a competitive work environment. Employers are impressed by students who accumulate a variety of paid and volunteer experiences through working in different sectors of society and with individuals from a broad range of ages. This diversity in training helps students become more qualified and gives them insight into which careers they are best suited for and which they would be best to avoid.

Star Student: Susan

Susan is a great example of a student who took good advantage of internship opportunities available to her. As part of her course work in Aging and Physical Activity, Susan visited a retirement community near her university where the class was conducting a research project. During this visit Susan got to know the activities director at the retirement community, and this contact led to a volunteer position running a strength-training program at the facility. Eventually the retirement community appreciated Susan's services so much that they hired her as a full-time activities coordinator. As her employer, they are now paying for her to complete a master's degree in kinesiology with the hope that she will continue to work for them for many years to come.

Susan, Master of Science in Kinesiology Student

© Human Kinetics

Pursue Academic Excellence

One of the consequences of the evolution of kinesiology as a field of study has been a substantial increase in the academic rigor of degree programs. The days are past when programs that focused on sport and exercise were considered by some to be a "soft major" filled with easy, unchallenging courses. On the contrary, at many institutions kinesiology is a rigorous and challenging degree, attracting highly qualified applicants, many of whom are among the highest achievers in their high school classes. As increasing numbers of kinesiology students extend their education by going on to graduate school, it has never been more important for students to do well academically to maximize their career options.

Get Involved in Research

Faculty at many universities and colleges are engaged in research projects funded by national research agencies or foundations. Sometimes these research projects provide opportunities for undergraduate students to get their first exposure to research. Many universities have undergraduate research programs in which students work shoulder to shoulder with professors in conducting research and then in presentations describing the roles they have played in the process. This research can encompass an astonishing variety of topics. A recent undergraduate research symposium at the University of Illinois featured the work of over 150 undergraduate students from more than 50 departments. Undergraduate research and both scholarly and creative activity were presented in several formats, including oral presentations, posters, and creative performances, including many presentations from kinesiology students. Projects ranged from laboratory-based exercise science experiments to community-based participatory research in conjunction with the local parks and recreation district.

Students who participate in research projects as undergraduates benefit significantly from their early exposure to the rewards and challenges associated with scientific research, and from the opportunity to work closely with a professor on a project of mutual interest. I encourage undergraduate freshmen to get involved in research projects as much as they can. Simply talking to your favorite professors and inquiring about opportunities available in their labs can be all it takes to get started on your career as a researcher.

Build Professional Relationships During Your College Years

I advise freshmen students to ask for paid trips to a national or regional conference of a professional society in their area of interest as a gift from parents or grandparents. Careers are often built and future decisions made based on informal interactions at conferences or professional meetings. I tell my freshmen about a former student who was an extraordinarily outgoing and personable young woman and a master at networking and building professional relationships. She was not an outstanding student academically, but she was truly exceptional at building social relationships. As a naturally shy person myself, I was always amazed at the way this young woman could introduce herself to strangers, striking up conversations about her research, her career goals, and her personal and professional interests. I was not at all surprised at the end of her studies when she had her choice of four or five positions in the leading laboratories in the country working under some of the major scholars in our field. The moral of this story is that it is never too soon to start building a professional network. The professor you meet at a state conference might well turn into your graduate school faculty mentor; the industry representative whose booth you visit could be your next boss. Acquiring the skills to network and interact in professional settings is one of the best investments students can make in their professional futures.

Supplement Kinesiology Courses With Diverse Electives

One outcome of the increasingly multidisciplinary nature of knowledge in kinesiology is that those in the field of kinesiology are called on to have a broader range of knowledge and skills. For this reason I encourage students to take as wide a range of electives as possible to maximize their flexibility in the employment market. If you are interested in a major in fitness and wellness, perhaps your university offers an undergraduate interdisciplinary major or minor that enables you to take courses in kinesiology, nutrition, counseling, and psychology, and to supplement this core with a range of electives. If you are considering sport management as a career, you might benefit from taking courses in the school of business or recreation, if your department allows electives in these areas. If you think you might want to be a physical education teacher, you will find interdisciplinary courses already embedded in your course of studies from education and perhaps biology, chemistry, and other sciences. Regardless of whether you select courses in traditional kinesiology degree programs or in more innovative hybrid programs combining courses from several departments, the message is clear: kinesiology graduates who wish to succeed in an increasingly diversified market place benefit from securing both a sound foundation in kinesiology as well as a wide exposure to knowledge from related fields.

As you can see, a number of issues are related to making intelligent career choices within the field of kinesiology. Kinesiology students today have an unprecedented variety of career choices available to them. The evolution of kinesiology into an evidence-based science has given the next generation of kinesiologists many opportunities, along with many challenges. Changes in our understanding of the nature of the relations among physical activity, sport, health, and quality of life require that future kinesiologists be more broadly educated than ever before and have sufficient background and experience to effectively partner with colleagues from numerous other disciplines. As more and more kinesiology students extend their education into graduate school, it has never been more important for undergraduates to excel academically in order to maximize their career options.

Chapter 3

Careers in Fitness Instruction, Personal Training, and Fitness Management

Warren Franke, PhD

According to many surveys, anywhere from 40 to 50 percent of all Americans do not get enough physical activity to maintain good health. About 60 percent of Americans are overweight, over 25 percent of them have high blood pressure, and 37 percent have high cholesterol. Almost 24 million Americans have diabetes, and over 5 million of them don't know it. In 2006, 80 million Americans had some form of cardiovascular disease, and 865,000 people died of it. *All* of these chronic conditions can be improved or even avoided through regular physical activity.

There has never been a better time than now to consider a career in fitness. In this chapter we look at a variety of fitness careers. We will discuss them separately, but many of them overlap. For example, personal trainers are often also employed as group exercise instructors. Both personal trainers and group exercise instructors might work with a wide range of people, and each might present the fitness instructor with different challenges. A 20-year-old college student and a 75-year-old client might both want to improve their fitness, but the types of physical activities a personal trainer prescribes for the two might be far different. This kind of variety makes a fitness career both exciting and challenging—because every client you work with is different from the last one.

Now let's look in depth at the many careers available in fitness instruction, personal training, and fitness management.

PERSONAL TRAINER

A personal trainer's primary responsibility is to help clients progress toward their fitness goals. The trainer usually accomplishes this by working one on one with clients, developing exercise programs specifically for them and targeted to their fitness goals and needs. The trainer then supervises clients as they work out, motivating them to continue exercising and modifying their programs as needed so they can continue to progress toward their goals.

Where You Will Work

Personal trainers work in many settings. Some are self-employed, working out of their home and travelling to clients' residences to train them. Some are employed at fitness facilities located at colleges, hospitals or medical clinics, corporations, nonprofit organizations such as YMCAs, or commercial fitness centers. Each of these affiliations brings a particular flavor to the job because the focus of each facility differs slightly from another, and the types of people attracted to the facility might differ as well. For example, on-campus fitness facilities usually attract, and are oriented to, people who have some connection to the college—students, alumni, faculty, staff, and other employees. A medically based clinic might provide services to relatively healthy members but might also provide exercise classes designed specifically for members with special needs such as arthritis, diabetes, or heart disease. Company-based facilities focus primarily, if not exclusively, on its employees. For example, employees of the Lands' End company have exclusive access to an 80,000-square-foot fitness center. YMCAs, with a primary mission of providing community services, usually offer fitness programs in fairly well-equipped fitness centers. However, not all of the 2,700 YMCAs in the United States have fitness centers. Whether or not a YMCA has a fitness center or fitness-focused programming often depends on the location of the Y; in some cities or neighborhoods, the Y isn't large enough to provide a fitness center, or other services are more critical to the neighborhood. Of the YMCAs that do sponsor fitness centers, the breadth and range of the offerings—including personal training—can vary considerably.

Most personal trainers are employed in commercial fitness centers. This is not surprising because there are a *lot* of fitness clubs. According to the International Health, Racquet and Sportsclub Association (IHRSA), there were about 33,000 fitness clubs in the United States in 2009. As with all businesses, commercial fitness centers exist to generate a profit. Personal trainers play an important part in this; recent information from IHRSA suggests that about 10 percent of revenue for most fitness centers comes from personal training services. In some fitness centers, that number is closer to 20 percent.

Salaries of personal trainers vary widely. Based on data from across the United States, the typical salary for personal trainers ranges from $20 to $40 per hour in

U.S. dollars, or about $30,000 to $40,000 annually. These dollar amounts represent median salaries—meaning they are the middle of the range of what trainers earn. Some might make considerably more or less than these amounts. Some of the factors that affect salary are unique to the fitness industry, and some are not. Personal trainers with college degrees who have certifications from accredited professional organizations along with several years of experience will usually earn higher salaries than those who do not. Self-employed personal trainers often make more money than trainers employed by a fitness center. Additionally, geographic regions affect salaries. For example, personal trainers in New York can expect to make more than personal trainers in Texas, according to a national survey conducted by the American Council on Exercise.

Self-employed personal trainers, meaning those trainers who either have their own exercise facility or train clients in the clients' homes, typically make more on an hourly basis than personal trainers working for a company. Self-employed trainers usually charge up to $50 an hour for their services, although some charge considerably more. In affluent areas where clients are willing to pay more, trainers might charge as much as $150 to $200 an hour. Although these incomes are great, they are *not* typical. Remember also that from this income the trainer must pay for all expenses associated with running a business, such as advertising, liability insurance, personal insurance, travel expenses, and taxes. Thus the net income of the trainer might be half of the gross income. Moreover, self-employed trainers usually don't enjoy a regular 8 to 5 work day because many clients want to train either before or after their own work day. So, a self-employed personal trainer might work with clients 8 hours over a given day, but these hours might span 12 or more clock hours.

Many self-employed personal trainers work on commission. In such cases, trainers might provide their services to clients at fitness centers. The fee paid by the client is split between the personal trainer and the fitness center. The amount of commission varies from center to center; generally, the more clients a trainer works with, the more money both the trainer and the fitness center can earn. Thus the client base is very important, and the size of this base typically depends on the skills and abilities of the trainer. Because self-employed personal trainers working with individual clients must arrange their work schedules to match those of their clients, their work week can vary considerably. Some clients will want to meet early in the morning before they go to work, and others will want to meet late in the afternoon after their workday ends. Others might want to meet in the middle of the day or over the weekend.

Some personal trainers are employed by fitness clubs, working either on a salary or hourly basis. Some clubs also allow their personal trainers to work on commission. Of the fee charged to the client, the trainer usually keeps about $25 per hour (U.S.) with the remainder going to the fitness club. Trainers employed by fitness centers without a complementary commission practice can expect to earn approximately $11 per hour. Thus the trainer who works on an hourly basis might earn less money than the self-employed trainer but also is likely to work more regular hours, ensuring a more regular income. Of course the work week of trainers, like all fitness center employees, depends on the hours of operation of the center. If a club is open from 5 in the morning until midnight, employee work schedules must be adjusted accordingly. Consequently, personal trainers rarely work a 40-hour week, and virtually none of them works a typical 8 to 5 schedule Monday through Friday.

What You Will Do

Unlike most of the other careers described in this chapter, personal trainers work on a one-on-one basis with their clients. Thus they usually develop a close working, and sometimes personal, relationship with those they are trying to help. In fact, personal trainers might be thought of as exercise counselors. Personal training might be the most personally demanding, and personally rewarding, job in a fitness center.

But what does a personal trainer actually do? In a nutshell, the trainer helps each client achieve the health or fitness goals that are in the client's best interests. Clients might have very specific goals, such as wanting to bench press 150 or 250 pounds or be able to run a 10K race in under 40 minutes, but usually the goals are more general, such as simply wanting to get in better shape. Some clients might engage a personal trainer because they want to reduce their risk for chronic diseases such as hypertension (high blood pressure), diabetes (lowering blood sugar), osteoporosis and arthritis, obesity, or heart disease. A well-educated, knowledgeable personal trainer can help the client develop an exercise plan to address these specific issues. Trainers also make recommendations to clients about other lifestyle changes needed to achieve their goals. For example, an exercise program is a very important part of any weight loss program. However, many, many studies have shown that an exercise program alone will most likely not lead to losing a lot of weight—a change

Factors Affecting Personal Trainer Salaries

1. Whether you are certified by an appropriate professional organization.*
2. How much experience you have.*
3. Whether you have a college degree in a related field, such as kinesiology.
4. If certified, whether you have additional certifications for "special" groups, such as those needing weight loss.
5. Whether you are an employee of a company, work on commission, or are entirely self-employed.
6. The type of company you work for (corporate, for-profit, hospital-based, etc.).
7. The region of the United States you live in.

*These were considered the two most important in a survey of personal trainers by the American Council on Exercise in 2006.

in eating habits is also required. Consequently, trainers might suggest ways clients can alter their lifestyles to achieve their weight-loss goals.

Trainers must be sufficiently knowledgeable of exercise physiology and anatomy and diagnostic methods so that they may accurately assess clients' fitness levels, analyze the results, and develop exercise programs. These tests can range from the very simple to the very complex. A simple test of cardiovascular endurance, for example, might be a 12-minute run; a complex test will involve a maximum-effort laboratory-based graded exercise test. A sit-up test might be used to determine muscular endurance, and a sit-and-reach test might be administered to assess flexibility. Based on these results, the personal trainer develops an exercise prescription, or a structured plan of exercise, designed to help clients achieve the goals they have set for themselves. The client and trainer then meet regularly as the personal trainer guides the client through his or her exercise program.

Whom You Will Work With

Fitness centers vary considerably in their mission and focus, but most offer relatively similar services—health risk assessments, fitness assessments, personal training and group fitness classes, and wellness education classes (such as weight-loss programs, diabetes classes, or stress-reduction classes). Frequently, personnel at fitness facilities team together to assist clients. For example, if a client would like to lose weight, a registered dietitian with extensive nutritional training might team up with a personal trainer to help the client achieve his or her goals. Personal trainers might also monitor a client's progress in classes and other activities. This might involve consulting group exercise instructors and others supervising the client's activities.

If the facility offers a broad array of services, special supervisors such as fitness directors, personal trainer supervisors, or exercise class coordinators might be on the staff. These specialists have responsibility for supervising the personal training staff, coordinating exercise class offerings, and, in general, ensuring that the fitness programs are well run. These supervisors usually have similar backgrounds to those of personal trainers or exercise instructors. However, they often have substantial work experience and an advanced degree, making them better prepared to supervise other employees. Because fitness centers are businesses, personnel with expertise in business will also be employed. These careers fall under fitness management (see Fitness Center Owner or Manager on page 42).

What Personal Skills and Abilities You Will Need to Succeed

Personal training requires many of the same skills and abilities needed by teachers because personal trainers often take on the role of a teacher. Both impart information; both are successful when their clients have learned what they need to know. Trainers motivate clients, just as teachers motivate students. Just like teachers, personal trainers must have a passion for their subject (exercise) and for helping others. They must be knowledgeable about exercise and training but, at the same time, be open to learning new things, realizing that there are always new exercise techniques and programs being developed. Patience is needed to help clients who are struggling to achieve difficult goals, and personal trainers also must be good listeners. As in any service-oriented profession, friendliness is critically important; if you are uncomfortable working face to face in a close relationship with other people, you probably would not be happy working as a personal trainer.

Of course personal trainers must be knowledgeable about exercise. This includes knowing how to use and adapt exercise equipment to clients' needs. If a client wants to improve his or her balance, the personal trainer must know whether foam rollers, Airex pads, BOSU, wobble boards, Versa discs, stability balls, or a combination of these are best suited for the client. If strength training is the goal, personal trainers must determine whether floor exercises, machine weights, free weights, resistabands, or medicine balls are most appropriate. Much like a professional carpenter, the trainer needs to have a "toolbox" of equipment along with the skill and expertise to know when to use each particular tool.

Like good teachers, personal trainers also need to be good role models. The personal trainer should not only talk the talk but walk the walk. This doesn't mean a personal trainer should be a body builder or be able to run a marathon, but it should be readily apparent to clients that the personal trainer heeds his or her own advice. On the other hand, it is critical to recognize that walking the walk is *not* the most important aspect of being a good personal trainer. Just because a person exercises a lot does not mean he or she is qualified to be a personal trainer.

Deb Atkinson

Director of personal training at Ames Racquet and Fitness Center in Ames, Iowa

"The most important aspect of this job is connecting the art of working with people and the (exercise) science of training. The best exercise prescription involves not just the exercise sequence and choices, but that the person enjoys it and connects pleasure with it so he or she will repeat it."

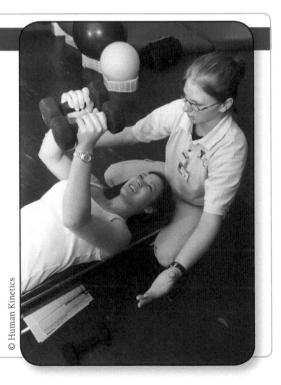

© Human Kinetics

What Education and Certifications You Will Need

An important factor that affects a personal trainer's salary is whether he or she has been certified by a creditable agency. It is absolutely critical to become certified as a personal trainer. Very few fitness centers hire uncertified personal trainers. The personal trainer's certification, like a teacher's or physician's license, ensures clients that the trainer has passed a rigorous set of examinations. In addition, certification offers some protection to a facility in the event a law suit is brought against it by a client. If a client is injured during an exercise session, any legal action brought against the facility or trainer might be mitigated somewhat (provided no negligence has been committed) by the credentials of the trainer.

Many certifications are available to trainers; unfortunately, many of them can be earned by attending little more than a few hours of class. Table 3.1 lists the most prestigious certifications, the organization providing the certification, and the minimum qualifications needed to take the certification examination. This list is not all-inclusive but does include all the organizations that have been accredited by the National Commission for Certifying Agencies (NCCA), an independent organization that certifies professional organizations and ensures that they have met a series of standards developed by the NCCA. The most sought after certifications require examinations that assess the applicant's scientific and factual knowledge as it relates to exercise *as well as* the applicant's ability to apply that knowledge in typical job situations. The certifications offered by the American College of Sports Medicine, the American Council on Exercise, and the National Strength and Conditioning Association are the most well regarded by many fitness experts.

A college program in kinesiology will ground you in the scientific basis of exercise, physiology, psychology, biomechanics, and motor development, but it probably will not provide you with the range of experience required to be a first-rate trainer. The more hands-on experience you can accumulate, the more skilled you will be. To facilitate this, the better undergraduate kinesiology programs require all students preparing for careers in the fitness industry to complete an internship experience at a fitness center for 10 or 12 weeks where their work is mentored by an employee. Most students will also benefit from part-time employment at a local fitness center while they are still in school. Even if you are not employed as a personal trainer, the experience will give you a feel for working in a fitness center environment and help you land a job when you graduate.

Finally, would-be personal trainers should affiliate with a relevant professional organization as early as possible. Doing so enables you to network with other interested professionals as part of attending meetings and conferences; it will also help you stay current in your education. Membership in most organizations brings with it a journal, or trade magazine, discounted fees for their professional meetings, and reduced rates for their certification exams. Many of the agencies listed in table 3.1 offer memberships; the most prestigious is the American College of Sports Medicine's Alliance of Health and Fitness Professionals. Another highly regarded organization is the IDEA Health and Fitness Association.

Table 3.1   Certification Programs*

Certifying agency	Certifications offered (some offer more certifications than listed here)	Requirements for certification
Academy of Applied Personal Training Education	Certified personal fitness trainer	• A high school diploma or equivalent • A human anatomy course or active status personal training certification
American College of Sports Medicine	Certified personal trainer	• 18 years of age • A high school diploma or equivalent • Current adult CPR certification with a practical skills component (such as the American Heart Association or American Red Cross)
	Health fitness specialist	*Minimum Requirements as of July 1, 2011:* • BA in kinesiology, exercise science, or other exercise-based degree • Current adult CPR certification with a practical skills component (such as the American Heart Association or American Red Cross)
American Council on Exercise	Personal trainer	• 18 years of age • Current adult CPR and AED certificate
	Group fitness instructor	• 18 years of age • Current adult CPR and AED certificate
	Lifestyle and weight-management consultant	• 18 years of age • Current adult CPR and AED certificate One of the following: • Current ACE personal trainer, group fitness instructor or advanced health and fitness specialist certification *OR* • NCCA-accredited personal trainer or advanced fitness-related certification *OR* • A four-year degree in an exercise science or related field at the time of registration *and* submit documentation supporting completion of exercise science–related coursework
	Advanced health and fitness specialist	• Same as lifestyle and weight management consultant *AND* • 300 hours of work experience designing and implementing exercise programs for apparently healthy individuals or high-risk individuals, as documented by a qualified professional
The Cooper Institute	Certified personal trainer	• 18 years of age • Current adult CPR and AED certificate
International Fitness Professionals Association	Certified personal fitness trainer	• Current CPR certificate
National Academy of Sports Medicine	Certified personal trainer	• 18 years of age • Current adult CPR and AED certificate
National Council on Strength and Fitness	Certified personal trainer	• 18 years of age • A high school diploma or equivalent • A minimum level of practical experience working in the health and fitness field recommended but not required
National Exercise and Sports Trainer Association	Certified personal fitness trainer	• 18 years of age • A high school diploma or equivalent • Exercise science background recommended • CPR certification recommended but not required

Certifying agency	Certifications offered (some offer more certifications than listed here)	Requirements for certification
National Exercise Trainers Association	Certified personal trainer	• 18 years of age (or parental consent) • CPR certification
	Certified group exercise instructor	• 18 years of age (or parental consent) • CPR certification
National Federation of Professional Trainers	Certified personal trainer	• 18 years of age • A high school diploma or equivalent • At least two years of practical, hands-on experience in weight/resistance training or cardio training • CPR certification recommended but not required
National Strength and Conditioning Association	Certified personal trainer	• 18 years of age • A high school diploma or equivalent • Current CPR and AED certification with a practical skills component (such as the American Heart Association or American Red Cross)
	Certified strength and conditioning specialist	• BA degree or chiropractic medicine degree • CPR and AED certification with a practical skills component (such as the American Heart Association or American Red Cross)
Training and Wellness Certification Commission	Advanced certified personal trainer	• Either a 500-hour State Board of Education approved training program OR a BA in a health-related field • Minimum of 200 hours of practical experience • Current CPR and AED certification with a practical skills component (such as the American Heart Association or American Red Cross)

*Accredited by the National Commission for Certifying Agencies as of September 2009.

Future Outlook

Although it is very hard to predict precisely what the future holds for employment opportunities in any field, the outlook for the fitness industry as a whole appears quite good. The U.S. Bureau of Labor Statistics predicts that the number of fitness jobs will grow much faster than the average of all occupations over the next 10 years. The current economic slowdown has affected fitness centers like most places of employment. As a result, people who can play multiple roles are likely to be in the most demand. For example, someone who can work one on one as a personal trainer, lead group exercise classes, and perform fitness assessments will have a leg up on those who can play only one or two roles. Again, the smart move is to gain as much and as broad a range of experience as you can.

Personal training is not the only career in the fitness industry. As we explore these, you will see that most careers, such as group exercise instructor, corporate/government/military fitness instructor, and strength and conditioning coach, require many of the same abilities as personal training demands. However, some, such as those related to managing or owning a fitness center, require an entirely different kind of expertise. It is up to you to decide which career appeals to you most.

GROUP EXERCISE INSTRUCTOR

Group exercise instructors differ from personal trainers in that they work with groups of exercisers rather than one on one with individual clients. As you will learn in this chapter, excellent group exercise instructors have a skill set just as unique as that of personal trainers.

Where You Will Work

Generally, group exercise instructors work in the same locales as personal trainers, although almost always in an established facility and rarely at clients' homes. The type of facility can vary considerably—it may be a fitness center, a worksite wellness program, a medically oriented center, or some other locale. The demographics of the clientele will probably also vary depending on the type of exercise class being taught. Larger fitness clubs tend to have a significant number of exercise instructors. For example, Aspen Athletic Clubs offers exercise classes at three of their locations in Des Moines, Iowa. In a typical week, over 40 different instructors teach more than 135 exercise classes!

Rightly or wrongly, leading group exercise classes tends to be viewed as less challenging than working as a personal trainer and, unfortunately, this perception is often reflected in the salary. Across the United States, group exercise instructors typically earn about $5 less per hour than personal trainers earn, or about $2,000 to $5,000 less per year. Geography plays a part in this. According to the American Council on Exercise, full-time group instructors earn more than personal trainers in the Northwest, about the same in the Northeast, and less elsewhere. In many fitness facilities, group exercise instructors also serve as personal trainers. Consequently, the annual income of an employee can vary considerably, depending on the total number of clients the specialist is serving.

What You Will Do

Many years ago, group exercise instructors were called aerobics instructors because virtually all the group exercise classes offered by fitness centers were just that—cardiovascular conditioning classes taught to music. Today the classes taught in fitness facilities are much more varied. They likely include step exercise, aquatic exercise, stationary cycling (spinning), weightlifting (Les Mills' Bodypump), dance (Zumba), combative arts (boxing, kickboxing), functional fitness (sport skills and movements), balance training (BOSU, stability aids), yoga, and Pilates. A single exercise class might include several of these activities; for example, a "cardiomix" class might consist of traditional aerobic class activities, BOSU ball work, functional fitness movements, and conclude with floor work focusing on core strength development. However, the basic makeup of a group exercise class has not changed from the early days of aerobics classes—one instructor leading a group of clients through a series of exercise activities, often using music either as part of the choreography or as background, regularly calling out instructions, with clients following his or her lead. Historically, clients have been predominantly women, and women still make up about two thirds of participants.

In virtually all fitness centers, exercise classes are held at regularly scheduled times; weekly class schedules that list the instructor are often posted weeks in advance. Consequently, group instructors can rely on a fairly regular work schedule, whereas personal trainers might have to adjust their work times on short notice to accommodate the client schedules. But just like personal trainers, the work schedule of exercise instructors is rarely a "normal" 40-hour work week. Many exercise classes must be offered either before or after normal office hours to accommodate the schedules of clients who have full-time jobs. Fitness centers are often busiest early in the morning and after 5:00 PM. Of course some exercise classes are offered during regular business hours to appeal to stay-at-home parents or retirees. For example, SilverSneakers, a program offered by some fitness clubs or recreation centers, provides a series of exercise classes oriented specifically to older adults. These classes are often offered midmorning—after employed clients have gone to work and retirees have had breakfast.

Whom You Will Work With

Exercise instructors generally do not perform fitness assessments, offer individual fitness counseling, or develop customized exercise programs. This doesn't mean they ignore the problems of individuals enrolled in their classes. They often direct them to others in the health and fitness or medical community who might meet their needs. In some fitness centers, members are permitted to drop into any exercise class at any time. If the class is large, these drop-ins might remain virtual strangers to the instructor. Consequently, group exercise instructors often do not enjoy the give and take that occurs between a personal trainer and a client. This also poses a dilemma for a group instructor. Kristen Maughan, an instructor who has taught classes for people ranging in age from 20 to 90 years, says, "In a group fitness class, there is often a wide range of fitness levels among members. The biggest challenge is being able to offer a variety of exercises that can be modified to fit any fitness level. You must be able to challenge those who are very fit while, at the same time, helping those who are less fit feel successful."

What Personal Skills and Abilities You Will Need to Succeed

Many of the skills and abilities important in personal training are also important in group exercise instruction. Possessing good people skills might be the most important of these; to do this type of work, you must genuinely like to be around and interact with people. Much like teaching, leading an exercise class is a performance. This is not a job for shy, introverted people! Exercise instructors must also possess good oral communication skills, including the ability to give very clear instructions in succinct phrases. You must have a strong voice that projects over the music. You must be well organized so that you can seamlessly transition from one exercise routine to another. Because most group exercise classes use music as cues for the exercise routines, it is important that you like to move your body, and are reasonably good at it (you should at least be able to keep a beat). Finally, you must be in excellent physical condition because group instructors participate in the classes they are leading. The exercise instructor that is too out of breath to give instructions to the class will not be a group exercise instructor for long!

What Education and Certifications You Will Need

As with personal trainers, employers prefer to hire group exercise instructors who have the appropriate education, certifications, and experience. Clients are most attracted to instructors who can offer well-designed, well-choreographed, and well-taught exercise classes. Consequently, employers often will hire group instructors with a wealth of experience but who lack a college degree rather than a person who has a degree but lacks experience. This doesn't mean that a degree in kinesiology isn't important. It is, for a number of reasons. It will make you more knowledgeable about the science of exercise, and you'll be able to use that knowledge to develop more effective exercise routines. Second, the type of knowledge gained in a kinesiology curriculum is a requisite for passing the more prestigious certification exams. Work experience alone is not enough to pass the more rigorous exams. Having both a degree and a certification will enhance your marketability. Third, as in any profession, possessing a college degree will give you opportunities for advancement. It is important to recognize that group exercise instructors, like professional athletes, face the prospect of not being able to work late into life because of the physical demands the job places on their bodies. Having a degree in kinesiology and years of experience as an exercise instructor often is the key to opening doors to other careers in the fitness industry.

For the same reasons that it is beneficial for a personal trainer to consider joining a professional organization, group exercise instructors should join as well. As with personal trainers, ACSM's Health and Fitness Alliance is probably the most beneficial. Membership includes a subscription to a useful journal, *ACSM's Health & Fitness Journal*, which provides helpful tips and insights from professionals. Membership in a professional organization and subscribing to trade journals will help you stay current in your field. A further way to continue your education is by attending professional meetings or taking continuing education classes. ACSM has an annual meeting, the Health & Fitness Summit, and the American Council on Exercise and the IDEA Health and Fitness Association offer a wide variety of conferences, courses, and publications to help you maintain your expertise.

Future Outlook

As is the case for personal trainers, the outlook for group exercise instructors is bright. A recent survey by the Sporting Goods Manufacturing Association found that participation in many types of group exercise classes has had double-digit growth over the past few years. For example, participation in spinning classes has increased

45 percent since 2000, whereas cardio kickboxing has increased 20 percent since 2008. Likewise, in a survey of over 41,000 people in 2009, the Physical Activity Council found that participation in high-impact aerobics increased by more than 8 percent, and low-impact aerobics increased by 6 percent over the past year. Thus, demand for personal trainers and group exercise instructors is high and, according to the U.S. Bureau of Labor Statistics, is expected to increase much faster than other occupations—over 20 percent—within the next 10 years.

A cautionary note for group exercise instructors is that they often find it difficult to land or maintain a full-time job in a fitness center. Because fitness training has become so specialized, it is nearly impossible for one person to develop the expertise needed to teach the wide variety of group exercise classes that fitness centers typically offer. Also, a full-time position involving 40 hours of exercise teaching and performing each week would be physically exhausting. For these reasons, fitness centers prefer to hire "utility persons" who can do more than one job. This is why so many group instructors are also personal trainers.

STRENGTH AND CONDITIONING COACH

Like personal trainers and group exercise instructors, strength and conditioning coaches help others to improve their fitness. But strength and conditioning coaches differ from the others in one very important way—the clients they work with are focused on improving their performance or skill in a sport. This is why strength and conditioning coaches work primarily with athletes.

Where You Will Work

With advances in the science of human performance, nearly all coaches have come to recognize the advantages of conditioning in high-level competition. This means strength and conditioning coaches are important contributors to most athletic teams. A strength and conditioning facility at a university resembles a fitness center but has significantly more weightlifting equipment because strength and power are crucial to success for most athletes. Conditioning coaches might also be employed by high schools, fitness centers, physical therapy clinics, and professional sport teams. They are increasingly employed by commercially based performance-enhancement companies such as the nationally franchised Velocity Sports Performance or Athletic Republic, or by locally owned centers such as Dynamic Sports Performance in Asburn, Virginia, or Proehlific Park in Greensboro, North Carolina. In this latter category of employers, the facility is likely to provide a range of equipment for improving agility, speed, and sport-specific performance.

Salaries for strength and conditioning coaches vary as much as the type of work they do; generally salaries are in the same range as those of personal trainers—typically in the $40,000 to $60,000 (U.S.) range depending on experience and qualifications. Most strength and conditioning coaches aspire to work at the college or professional level. Head conditioning coaches at the college level are typically paid anywhere from $45,000 to $75,000 annually. Some can earn as much as $200,000, but these higher salaries are rare. Conditioning coaches for professional teams typically earn more than college coaches, but usually less than $100,000 per year.

What You Will Do

Strength and conditioning coaches have two primary goals. The first is to improve athletic performance, which usually means improving athletes' speed, strength, and power (although specifics vary according to athlete and sport). Conditioning coaches develop systematic training programs for both teams and individual athletes, often working in close association with coaches. This usually includes teaching proper lifting techniques, supervising and motivating athletes as they work out, and assessing their performance before and after the program. The nature of the conditioning program will vary depending on whether the sport is in season or not. During the off-season, conditioning programs can be quite rigorous. In season, conditioning programs tend to focus more on maintaining athletes' conditioning than on improving it. Conditioning programs also vary by sport, and even by position within the sport.

The second primary goal is to reduce athletic injuries. To that end, conditioning coaches often design regimens to strengthen body parts that are prone to injury in a particular sport. Andrew Moser, Strength Coach at Iowa State University agrees,

Andrew Moser

Director of strength and conditioning for Olympic sports in the department of athletics at Iowa State University

In describing the most important qualities for strength and conditioning coaches, Moser notes that "it is important to have a great educational background and knowledge in strength and conditioning. However, some of the biggest qualities that you need to have are being able to communicate, motivate, and relate to various people—all with different personalities. You can have all the knowledge out there, but if you can't apply that knowledge to designing a program that works for your student-athletes and can't communicate that information to your athletes and coaches, it is not going to do you much good."

Photo courtesy of Andrew Moser.

saying, "Student-athletes can have a great training plan that improves their speed, agility, strength, explosiveness, etc., but if we can't keep them healthy and out there competing, then all of the training improvements don't help us." Thus to prevent athletes from getting injured during training, conditioning coaches must know the correct exercise and lifting techniques and be able to teach them to athletes. The conditioning coach also monitors athletes' general health, sometimes providing nutritional advice or referring athletes to a registered dietitian if they need more sophisticated nutritional counseling.

Whom You Will Work With

In ideal environments, athletic departments hire one conditioning coach for every 10 to 20 athletes who use the conditioning facility. The actual number of coaches is usually much less. Depending on the size of the athletic program and the level of competition, there might be as few as one or two conditioning coaches. The University of Notre Dame has 9 full-time coaches who work with about 750 student-athletes. Iowa State University has 4 full-time coaches for about 450 student-athletes. Central College in Pella, Iowa, competes at the NCAA division III level and, despite also having about 450 student-athletes, only recently hired a second full-time conditioning coach. At the professional level, you usually find more coaches working with fewer athletes. For example, the Washington Redskins have three coaches for about 75 athletes, and the San Antonio Spurs have a coach for 15 players.

Conditioning coaches usually meet regularly with the team's coaches to determine what individual athletes, or the team, needs to work on in the conditioning facility. If working with an injured athlete engaged in rehabilitation, conditioning coaches will also consult with the sports medicine or athletic training staff to be sure they do not ask the injured athlete to do anything inappropriate in the conditioning facility. Conditioning coaches who work in sport performance-enhancement facilities usually work with other performance specialists. Their client base tends to be younger (junior high school or senior high school students), and they interact often with their clients' parents.

What Personal Skills and Abilities You Will Need to Succeed

Athletic exercise programs can be fairly rigorous, and it can be difficult to get athletes to train as hard as they should. For this reason conditioning coaches must be good motivators. Because of the diversity of their clientele, coaches must be organized in how they administer each conditioning program and be detail oriented in terms of record keeping. Much like a personal trainer, a conditioning coach must be a good teacher because he will be trying to educate athletes on how to execute weightlifting and other exercises correctly. Conditioning coaches must also be perceptive; they will be monitoring athletes as they train, correcting any lifting errors they make. Finally, to work successfully with an array of athletes, coaches, and maybe even parents, the conditioning coach requires above-average interpersonal skills.

What Education and Certifications You Will Need to Succeed

Like any professional, a successful conditioning coach requires the right combination of education, certification, and experience. A conditioning coach should have at least a BA degree, with kinesiology as the ideal major. A master's degree is usually required for college-level jobs. There are many certifying agencies, but there is really only one widely respected certification for strength and conditioning coaches: the CSCS, or Certified Strength & Conditioning Specialist offered by the National Strength and Conditioning Association. This certification is virtually a requirement for employment as a conditioning coach.

Experience might be equally as important as preparation for a career as a conditioning coach. The wise student will gain firsthand experience in a strength and conditioning environment while still in college. Whether working as an assistant, an intern, or as a volunteer, nothing is more important than gaining firsthand experience. Working in a fitness center is helpful in this regard, but most fitness centers are committed to improving health and fitness rather than athletic performance. For this reason, it is also important to merge studies in kinesiology with experience working under the supervision, or mentoring, of a skilled strength and conditioning coach. Fortunately many coaches like to share their expertise with enthusiastic young people interested in pursuing similar careers. As is true for the other fitness careers discussed in this chapter, it is worthwhile to become a member of a professional organization. The premier organization for conditioning coaches is the National Strength and Conditioning Association. Members have access to several journals focusing on the science behind conditioning as well as practical methods of doing so.

Future Outlook

The job market for strength and conditioning coaches is brisk but tough. There is considerable competition for jobs, especially at the college and professional levels. Some strength and conditioning coaches hire assistants who have a good pedigree, meaning they have worked with well-known conditioning coaches in the past. It can be difficult breaking into this circle without having made connections or having proved yourself with top-level conditioning coaches. On the other hand, strength and conditioning expertise is becoming more sought after by performance-enhancement companies and fitness clubs. In a recent survey of worldwide fitness trends, the American College of Sports Medicine found that demand for strength-training experts was one of the top five most promising employment trends over the past few years. Note that this survey was administered primarily to fitness-oriented clubs and facilities, not athletic programs.

FITNESS CENTER OWNER OR MANAGER

The top job in the fitness industry is owner or manager of a center or facility. Those who aspire to this career must be willing to accept enormous responsibility and, because most fitness centers are for-profit operations, be interested and capable of running a business. Such positions are ideal for those who want to stay close to the action in the gym yet earn substantially more than they would in other types of fitness employment.

Where You Will Work

Commercial, or for-profit, fitness clubs comprise the largest number of facilities in the United States, followed by community-based programs (e.g., YMCA, hotel-based, community parks and recreation departments, colleges), corporate fitness centers and, last, medical- or hospital-based clinics. As is true in any business, the manager is the person in charge and usually earns the most. However, the manager also assumes most of the responsibility for the center's programs and activities. When the goal of an enterprise is to make money, the manager is responsible for ensuring it does so. Those managers who fail will not likely be employed for long.

General managers of fitness centers earn about the same as an in-demand personal trainers. More experienced managers, especially those in larger fitness centers and with 20 or more years of experience, typically earn a median salary of $45,000 to $75,000 (U.S.) annually, whereas managers with fewer than five years of experience might expect to earn around $25,000 to $45,000 per year. Of course, the owner of a popular, well-run facility can earn considerably more.

What You Will Do

General managers might or might not own the facility where they work. If they do not, they will probably work closely with the owner. The primary roles of the general manager are threefold: to promote the facility through advertising, marketing, and other membership drives; to manage business activities related to the facility, including the hiring of staff; and to make sure the programs offered by the center, such as exercise classes and other initiatives, are attractive to clients, relevant, and of a high quality. In short, the manager ensures that the fitness center operates as a well-run business.

Large facilities might hire several supervising managers, each with different responsibilities. It is typical, for example, for a fitness club to have a service manager, an operations manager, and sometimes a membership director. The service manager supervises the front desk and childcare services. The operations manager ensures the facility is well maintained, which usually means supervising the housekeeping and maintenance staff. If there is a membership director, his or her job is to supervise the sales staff and related programs. These business-oriented employees do not necessarily need any expertise in the personal training–side of the fitness center.

Responsibilities of managers can be quite diverse. For example, the service manager usually supervises the employees who work at the front desk. Because the front desk is the initial point-of-contact for all members and might be the basis for a customer's first impression, service managers are responsible for ensuring that staff are well trained in customer service etiquette. They are responsible for opening and closing the facility and for smoothly checking in members. They might also help with sales from a pro shop, control locker keys and locker rental, enforce facility rules and regulations (such as member dress code), use appropriate telephone-handling procedures, handle lost-and-found items, and be prepared to assist with emergencies (such as calling 911). The service manager thus has a big job, but it is all related to customer service; none of it relates to exercise instruction.

Whom You Will Work With

General managers work with diverse groups of people, including disgruntled customers, underperforming staff, and prospective customers. They attend regular meetings with service managers, fitness directors, operations managers, and accounting staff. General managers might conduct personnel evaluations that bring them directly into contact with all staff. Service and operations managers, in turn, interact with employees who are directly under their supervision.

What Personal Skills and Abilities You Will Need to Succeed

According to the online resource center for the International Health, Racquet and Sportsclub Association (the primary trade association serving health and fitness clubs), great managers have the following traits: "they know when to lead and when to follow, they recognize the value of the people who work for them, they make calculated decisions, they solve problems, they have vision, and, most important, they never stop learning."

General managers must be comfortable leading. Good leaders ensure that those who work for them know what is expected of them and share their professional values. They do not shy away from counseling, correcting, and even terminating staff when they fail to perform their assigned duties. Managers must have strong interpersonal skills; they must be good at handling information, keeping tabs on how things are functioning in all areas, and passing this information onto others (such as their boss). Managers are primary decision makers; they need good judgment and a great deal of common sense. They must also be observant. Many issues that arise in fitness centers occur because someone was not paying attention. For example, if a cable is frayed on a weightlifting machine, the cable must be replaced immediately to reduce the risk of someone being injured. If a frayed cable results in an injury, both the club and the manager could be liable for damages.

What Education and Certifications You Will Need

Most managers have college degrees; sometimes the degree is in business rather than kinesiology. Operations or service managers might have degrees in hotel and restaurant management or hospitality. Fitness center employees customarily work their way up the employment ladder based on job performance, personal skills, and abilities. Someone who excels in personal training might be promoted to fitness director; if they perform well in that job, they might eventually advance to general manager. Thus, as often happens in other types of employment, promotions may lead to positions in which the link between their college degree and their professional position is less distinct. Still, the experiences gained as a personal trainer or exercise leader makes one especially qualified as a manager, providing of course that the individual has also developed the appropriate business knowledge and skills to manage. So, fitness trainers and instructors who want to move into management must plan their careers to take advantage of supervisory and management responsibilities, however minor, along with any in-service educational opportunities that become available. Because of these advancement possibilities, some kinesiology programs require students to take some business-oriented coursework as they work toward their bachelor's degree.

Future Outlook

The fitness industry is a healthy business. According to the IHRSA, there are almost 30,000 health clubs in the United States with about 45 million members, 300,000 full-time employees, and 1.2 million part-time employees. Because almost 40 percent of the population of the United States is underexercised, the potential for new customers is enormous. On the other hand, the industry is extremely competitive and, consequently, centers are subject to the forces of a capitalistic market. So if you aspire to be a fitness manager or owner, you must thoroughly understand the business aspects of operating a fitness center in order to survive the market forces.

HEALTH PROMOTION SPECIALIST

The World Health Organization (WHO) defines health promotion as the "process of enabling people to increase control over their health and its determinants, and thereby improve their health." As the role played by physical activity in developing and maintaining health has become clearer in recent years, professional positions for kinesiologists as health promotion specialists have expanded. Their educational background and training equips them to offer input on how physical activity can be integrated with other features of a healthy lifestyle. Kinesiologists can be an important part of local, regional, and national health promotion efforts.

Where You Will Work

Health promotion specialists help others become more physically active. Unlike personal trainers and group exercise leaders, these specialists are more holistic in their approach, counseling clients and developing programs for groups of people with the larger health picture in mind. Health promotion specialists could be employed in any facility that hires a personal trainer or group exercise instructor or, like personal trainers, they might be self-employed. However, most of these specialists work as employees of a corporation, community-based agency, allied health facility, or health maintenance organization. Health promotion specialists are most commonly employed in worksite wellness programs. For example, the Principal Financial Group budgets almost $1.5 million for employee wellness, and about half of that is for personnel, some of whom are employed as health promotion specialists.

As with all the careers described in this chapter, the salary earned by these specialists depends on many factors, including education, experience, and certifications. The typical salary range is $30,000 to $45,000 (U.S.) but can be higher, even double this amount, if the specialist has a graduate degree, sufficient experience, appropriate certifications, and works for a large company.

What You Will Do

Like a personal trainer, a health promotion specialist helps clients succeed in achieving the goals of their exercise programs This might entail administering fitness assessments, developing exercise programs, and working with clients as they exercise. Unlike the trainer, however, the health promotion specialist focuses more on helping the client become healthier, not just fitter. Thus they work with clients on a broad range of health-related goals. For example, they might work with a client who is diabetic, overweight, inactive, under stress, and locked in a pattern of poor eating habits. As they help this client develop a program of physical activity, they might also help him or her make other lifestyle changes needed to lose weight, manage their diabetes, reduce their stress, and improve their dietary habits. As you can see, health promotion specialists are first and foremost counselors who help others become healthier.

If you are employed in a worksite wellness program, your primary responsibility is to help employees of the company become healthier. The advantages to companies of having a healthy workforce are many, including reduced absenteeism, lowered costs for company-provided health insurance, and a more productive workforce. In such cases, individual counseling of all employees might not be feasible, so it is likely you will also be responsible for planning company-wide initiatives, such as monthly newsletters, Internet-based programs, kiosk displays in the cafeteria, contests between different divisions of the company, and the like.

Whom You Will Work With

The nature of the position of health promotion specialist requires working with everyone, from the top managers of a company to the mail room clerks and custodians. Consequently, they must be able to relate to and communicate effectively with workers of all levels. Because health promotion specialists usually work in teams with other specialists (such as registered dieticians), a cooperative and collaborative disposition is required. Sometimes health promotion specialists consult with physicians and other medical professionals. Other collaborators might include staff in the company's marketing department, who might help design posters, displays, e-mailings, and other advertising as part of selling a health promotion initiative to employees. Health-promotion specialists might also meet regularly with the human resources department in an effort to determine the effectiveness of a particular company-wide health promotion program.

What Personal Skills and Abilities You Will Need to Succeed

Because they usually work with many groups of people and in many capacities, organizational skills are a must for these specialists. For the same reason, good communication skills are essential, because the same message might have to be presented in very different ways to different people. Charisma and good motivational skills are important, because convincing clients to make changes in their behaviors is central to the health promotion specialist's job. Listening skills are also critical; counseling others is as much listening as it is talking. As is the case for any professional occupation, an interest in self-betterment through continual learning is important for the fitness specialist. Because health-related recommendations are constantly being updated, it is particularly important for the fitness specialist to stay abreast of the latest developments.

What Education and Certifications You Will Need

A college degree in a health-related field is a must. Because of the diverse skills needed for the position, many companies prefer to hire someone with a master's degree. Students interested in this career path should consider supplementing their kinesiology degree program with coursework in community or public health. A course or two in techniques of counseling will improve skills integral to the job of fitness-promotion specialist. Because health-promotion specialists aim at changing the behavior of their clients, appropriate elective courses in psychology can also be helpful. In addition, skills in planning and "selling" company health-promotion initiatives to employees might be facilitated by coursework in marketing from the business school.

The certifications prescribed for a personal trainer or group exercise instructor will also be helpful to a fitness-promotion specialist because he or she will often work in exercise settings housed in corporations, hospitals, or fitness facilities. In addition to the certifications listed earlier in the chapter, those interested in a career as a health promotion specialist should consider earning the designation of certified health education specialist. The focus of this certification is on health education rather than fitness education. The required exam tests candidates' proficiency at assessing individual and community needs for health education, planning and implementing strategies and programs, and communicating and advocating for health and health education. A college degree with a strong emphasis in health education (perhaps as a second major or a minor) is required to take this examination.

> ## Other Fitness-Related Careers

By now you probably have a clear sense of the kinds of fitness-related careers available. However, what has been discussed thus far does not cover all the potential employment opportunities. Fitness-related careers can also be found in corporations, government facilities, and military bases. For the most part, these instructors work for an independent company that operates on a contractual basis with the corporation, government, or military. Like any contractor, fitness contractors are hired to provide a service for a fee; in turn, the contractor hires personnel and oversees the operation.

For example, the Washington, DC facility of the federal Bureau of Engraving and Printing provides a fitness center to 2,400 employees. In an effort to increase both employee use and services to the employees, they contracted with Aquila, Ltd. to manage the day-to-day operations of the facility as well as to provide wellness and fitness programs focused on reducing occupational injuries and increasing employee interest. Part of this arrangement included using Aquila fitness experts, such as those described in this chapter, to work with the employees onsite. Besides onsite management of a fitness facility, many companies can provide other, related, services. For example, Health Fitness Corporation works with companies to develop health promotion or occupational injury prevention programs. Thus, companies like Aquila and Health Fitness Corporation will continue to hire personal trainers, managers, fitness-promotion specialists and other occupations discussed in this chapter.

FITNESS LEADER IN GERONTOLOGY SETTINGS

The U.S. Administration on Aging estimates that the number of people 65 years of age or older will increase from 40 million in 2009 to 88 million in 2050. The number of people 85 or older will likely more than triple. Thus the demand for kinesiologists interested in working with older adults will remain quite strong. Physical activity benefits older adults by increasing strength, balance, cardiovascular fitness, and flexibility; it also helps older adults maintain their functional abilities, such as carrying out household chores, which enables them to remain independent. These benefits are even more important if the older adult has a chronic disease. Physical activity, it is often said, can help older adults *age in place* rather than being moved to an assisted-living facility or nursing home.

Where You Will Work

Because of the increasing number of older adults and the profound benefits of physical activity, more and more fitness centers are catering to elderly clients. For example, over 9,000 fitness centers in the United States now offer Silver Sneakers exercise classes, which is a fitness and health promotion program that provides memberships at qualified fitness centers to any eligible older adult. Also, more and more independent living and assisted-living facilities are building fitness centers and hiring staff as a service to the residents. Virtually all of the 497 active-aging businesses recently surveyed by the International Council on Active Aging, for example, indicated that having fitness facilities or wellness programming attracted more residents and made them less likely to move elsewhere. Because this niche in the fitness industry is relatively new, salary trends have not been tracked. However, salaries are likely comparable to those of personal trainers or exercise instructors—in the ballpark of $30,000 to $40,000 (U.S.). A fitness leader who has experience working with older adults may be able to negotiate a slightly higher salary.

What You Will Do and Whom You Will Work With

The skills that serve you well as a personal trainer or exercise instructor will also be of help to you as an exercise leader for older adults. The unique aspect of this career is the unique characteristics of the clientele. Older adults often are beset by a host of physical limitations, including arthritic joints, waning muscular strength and endurance, and limitations in flexibility. Although they might not be able to exercise as vigorously as younger adults, and their exercise programs must be designed with their medical conditions in mind, they most certainly can benefit from exercise. For example, although it takes longer, most older adults can increase their strength just as readily as younger adults. Thus a weight-training program designed for a 75-year- old client will incorporate the same training principles appropriate for someone much younger. Of course the 75-year-old likely has health issues that the younger client does not. Thus the trainer needs to modify exercise routines to take into account conditions such as arthritis, osteoporosis, or heart problems. Also, exercise programs for older adults typically include balance and mobility training. Falls are a major cause of injuries in this population, and training programs to improve balance have been shown to be effective in reducing the incidence of falls.

What Personal Skills and Abilities You Will Need to Succeed

In addition to the skills and abilities required for personal training, those who work with older adults must have a special gift for compassion, caring, and a desire to be supportive. A flair for creatively modifying exercises to accommodate clients' medical conditions is a must. Many older adults are reluctant to exercise, often claiming they are "too old." At many retirement centers, the largest crowds are assembled in front of the TV. Convincing an elderly person, or someone who might have become locked into a sedentary lifestyle over many years, that they can exercise is a challenge that requires creativity and motivational skills. A sense of humor is helpful, too, because older adults often respond better to light-hearted banter than to stern directions. Workers in this field need to be especially observant—watching their older clients carefully to be sure they are tolerating the exercise well and that they can perform it without injuring themselves.

What Education and Certifications You Will Need

A college education is a minimum requirement for this kind of work. Exercise leaders need to understand the physiological and psychological changes associated with aging and know how to adapt exercise to those changes when developing exercise programs. This type of information is almost impossible to obtain through on-the-job experience. Thus the ideal education for this position is a degree in kinesiology and a minor in gerontology.

Although information on "older adult personal trainer" certifications can be found on the Internet, none have been approved by the National Commission for Certifying Agencies. On the other hand, a group of professional fitness associations has assembled a list of competencies for older adult exercise professionals (see www.seniorfitness.net/National%20Standards.htm).

Future Outlook

The future for people who choose this career path is bright. As mentioned previously, older adults comprise the fastest-growing proportion of the U.S. population. This group is not only more affluent than their peers in the past, they tend to be more interested and knowledgeable about the role of fitness in maintaining health. They are more likely to be active than older adults of previous generations. Thus personal trainers and group exercise leaders with expertise in working with older adults will likely have an abundance of potential customers who can afford the trainers' services.

Chapter 4

Careers in Physical Education, Sport Instruction, Coaching, Sports Officiating, and Sport Psychology

Kim C. Graber

Thomas J. Templin

Rhonda Haag

Jamie O'Connor

Individuals who have been positively associated with physical activity, either as participants in physical education class or as athletes on a team, often elect to continue their association with physical activity by selecting a career as a physical education teacher, sport instructor, coach, sports official, or sport psychologist. Although each of these fields shares physical activity as a common denominator, each also has unique characteristics that make it different from the others. In some cases, individuals can successfully combine two career tracks, such as teaching and coaching at the high school level or instructing at a YMCA during the day and officiating at sporting events in the evening. In other cases, the demands of one career track are so substantial, such as coaching at the collegiate level or working as a sport psychologist for a professional team, that combining career tracks would be impossible. In these careers, the greatest challenge might be successfully balancing work and personal life. If you enjoy your job and look forward to going to work, however, trying to lead a well-balanced life can be a good problem to have.

PHYSICAL EDUCATION TEACHER

Are you someone who has been a camp counselor, park district employee, athlete, or youth sport coach? Do you enjoy interacting with children or teenagers and desire to positively influence young lives? Do you enjoy physical activity, physical education class, being an athlete on an interscholastic sport team, or engaging in activities in which you use your body to express yourself? If your answer to these questions is yes, you are probably well suited for a career as a physical education teacher.

Where You Will Work

Most certified physical education teachers work in public or private schools. Some prefer working with younger children and elect to teach in preschool or elementary schools. Others who enjoy older students or hope to coach often elect to teach at the middle-school or high-school level. Those who obtain master's and doctoral degrees often become instructors or professors at the college or university level. Whereas some prefer the public school environment, others opt to teach in private school settings. Interestingly, many individuals who think they might like to teach at one level change their minds after practicum teaching experiences provide them with new insights on the other levels of teaching.

Here's a quick synopsis of different settings in which physical education teachers work:

➤ **Preschool:** Although only a handful of individuals are currently employed as full-time physical education teachers at the preschool level, interest is growing in exposing young children to physical activity taught by a certified physical educator. If you opt to teach physical education at this level, you have the opportunity to help children acquire basic motor skills and develop a love of movement, but likely you will be asked to teach children in other capacities as well.

➤ **Elementary school:** Typically, children attend elementary school from kindergarten through fifth or sixth grade. Children at this age enjoy physical education and frequently list it as their favorite subject. Elementary physical education teachers are very lucky because they are one of the most beloved teachers in the school and have students who are eager to participate and engage in physical activity.

➤ **Middle school:** Children in middle school (sometimes called junior high) are at an interesting stage in their lives. Between childhood and adolescence, this age group welcomes physical education when it is perceived as fun. Physical education teachers who enjoy this level welcome the challenge of teaching students who are trying to decide whether participating in physical activity is cool or not.

➤ **High school:** Many physical education teachers select this level because they are also interested in coaching. The high school environment, however, can pose challenges that physical education teachers at the other levels don't experience. Many times teachers encounter adolescents who resist participating in physical activity because they don't want to get sweaty, believe they are low skilled, or don't want to expose their bodies by wearing a uniform. Although it is easy for high school physical education teachers to become frustrated, those who succeed are creative at encouraging participation, developing a curriculum that is effective and engaging, and forming a strong bond with their students. If you ultimately decide that you prefer teaching younger children, it is possible to teach at the elementary level while coaching at the high school level.

➤ **College or university:** A select number of physical education teachers attend graduate school for a master's and even a doctoral degree because they want to teach physical education at the college level or hope to educate future physical education teachers. Because most individuals decide to teach at this level only after several years of teaching at the elementary, middle, or high school levels, we won't focus on this level in this chapter.

➤ **Public schools:** The majority of certified physical education teachers are located in public schools. Because public schools are subsidized by federal and state taxes, their funding level generally reflects the national and state economy. According to the U.S. Bureau of Labor Statistics, in 2008 the median annual teacher salary ranged from $47,100 to $51,180 (U.S.). Beginning teachers earned an average of $33,227, and those with more years of experience made over $80,000. During a good economy, you will likely have smaller class sizes and access to better equipment. In times of a poor economy, physical education programs are sometimes reduced in size or eliminated in favor of funding subjects such as science and math. Thus it is to your advantage to obtain dual certification so you can also teach in another subject area, if necessary. Can you speak Italian? Do you enjoy math? How do you feel about teaching poetry? Also, because public schools are subject to property tax, those teaching in higher socioeconomic status areas will likely have higher salaries and better working conditions than those in lower socioeconomic status areas, such as lower income sections of large cities, where good teachers are often the most needed.

➤ **Private schools:** Although most private schools require you to be certified to teach physical education, some require no certification at all. Obviously, certification provides you with additional knowledge about teaching, so we recommend seeking certification even if you are planning to teach in a private school without certification requirements. Further, relocating to another position is difficult without proper certification credentials. Those who select private schools do so because class sizes are generally small and teachers usually experience few discipline problems. On the downside, salaries are often lower because they are not subsidized by tax dollars.

➤ **Other:** A small percentage of certified physical education teachers prefer a nonschool setting and seek employment at a park district, YMCA, or even as a whitewater rafting guide or mountain climbing instructor. Becoming a physical education teacher opens the door to many possibilities and forms of employment. Careers in less conventional settings are discussed later in the chapter.

What You Will Do

As a teacher, your primary responsibilities include curriculum development, lesson planning, and instruction. You will also be expected to contribute to the school community by attending faculty meetings, participating in inservice workshops, and periodically assisting in such capacities as lunchroom duty, hallway monitoring, and special event coordination.

➤ **Curriculum development:** Individuals who elect to become teachers often think of the actual instruction of students instead of more broadly about the many responsibilities for which a teacher is accountable. As a new teacher, you will most likely enter a school with an existing curriculum, which is a written guide that explains the overall curriculum over the course of a year for all grade levels within the school. For example, the elementary curriculum might emphasize teaching younger students about movement concepts and providing them with basic motor skills. The curriculum for high school students might be prescribed during the freshman year to include instruction in health and fitness, yet be an elective for juniors and seniors so they can select sports and activities that are interesting to them personally. As you gain experience, you will be responsible for reviewing the curriculum on a regular basis and periodically rewriting it to reflect a contemporary perspective.

➤ **Lesson planning:** Based on the overall curriculum, teachers are expected to write daily plans that include information about their objectives, lesson activities, teaching points, and learning standards. Teachers in their first year spend more time planning than at any other point in their career. Effective teachers reflect on the strengths and weaknesses of individual lessons and make notes so they will be more successful in subsequent teaching episodes.

➤ **Instruction:** Most physical education teachers find actual instruction the most enjoyable part of the job. This is when you are introducing students to new activities, explaining concepts, organizing students into groups, observing their performance, providing feedback, and instantly readjusting instruction based on students' needs and abilities. This is also the time in which you develop relationships and bonds with students. Depending on the school district in which you are teaching, you might have the luxury of instructing students on a daily basis or the challenge of visiting students once per week at multiple schools. Of course teachers who see their students more regularly can accomplish more, will learn students' names more easily, and better understand the needs of individual learners. Those with less regular contact encounter greater challenges but can experience satisfaction by introducing children to activities they find enjoyable and elect to pursue outside of the school setting because you have exposed them to that activity in physical education class.

➤ **Other responsibilities:** Physical education teachers must participate as integral members of the whole school community. The best and most highly respected teachers are those who exert their leadership to positively influence all members of the school's community. These teachers often volunteer to become the school

Star Student: Jessica

The student teaching internship is the best experience I could have had to prepare me to teach. The cooperating teacher is such a good resource to observe and interact with on classroom-management techniques. She has helped me learn about each student more quickly. As I gradually take on more responsibilities and have more control over teaching the lessons, I feel more and more competent to take over the classroom on my own.

Photo courtesy of Julia A. Valley.

Jessica (pictured on left in photo), K–8 physical education student teaching intern

activity leader. They frequently organize such events and programs as community walks, afterschool track-and-field meets, staff physical activity clubs, intramural programs, all-school fitness days, and equipment fund-raisers.

Whom You Will Work With

If you are located in a moderate- to large-sized middle or high school, your closest colleagues will consist of other physical education teachers. If you teach in an elementary school or smaller-sized secondary school, you are likely to be the only physical education teacher in the building. Although you might feel isolated at times, remember you have many classroom teachers with whom you can interact. Also, because you are the only physical education specialist, you have the advantage of being the individual whom others look to for leadership in physical activity. You might be motivated to develop a health and fitness center for staff or a school-wide classroom physical activity program.

The individuals with whom you will most frequently interact are children. Although at times they might be demanding of your attention, there is no greater reward than seeing the smile of a child who has learned a new skill or reading a letter from a grateful teenager whom you helped through a difficult personal problem.

What Personal Skills and Abilities You Will Need to Succeed

Think of your favorite physical education teachers. What qualities made them successful? Effective teachers have many positive traits, but four attributes that we believe are vital to a teacher's success are enthusiasm, flexibility, sensitivity, and commitment.

➤ **Enthusiasm:** Successful teachers are passionate about their career; they look forward to work, have an infectious enthusiasm for the subject matter, and lead a physically active lifestyle. They inspire their colleagues to constantly improve the curriculum, advocate for their subject matter, are good role models, and are concerned that children learn from their lessons. They are excited to teach, eager to respond to the needs of learners, and happily assume additional responsibilities. Students are drawn to their classes and enjoy participating.

➤ **Flexibility:** At times physical education teachers are challenged and required to show flexibility. For example, you might have planned to teach an aerobic dance routine in the main gym only to discover that a school assembly has been scheduled at the last minute. You have two options. The first option is to become frustrated that other events seem to take precedence over physical education. Your second option is to be flexible and find an alternative activity that is equally educational. Teachers who elect the second option have a positive conversation with school administration so that they are alerted, when possible, in advance of disruptive events and can plan accordingly.

➤ **Sensitivity:** Physical education teachers are required to respond to incidents that range from physical injury to name-calling. In all cases, they must exhibit sensitivity and good judgment. They must be sympathetic to the child who is physically injured after a fall or is emotionally upset because he or she is having difficulty acquiring a new skill. They also must be respectful of individual student differences such as gender, race, ability, size, and even interest in the subject matter. They must be sensitive to issues of bullying and not tolerate the behaviors of children who show disrespect toward each other.

➤ **Commitment:** Effective teachers demonstrate high commitment by being good role models, acting responsibly (e.g., punctual, professionally dressed, well-planned), and participating themselves as lifelong learners. They attend professional conferences, remain updated by reading professional articles, are knowledgeable about many activities, and assume professional leadership positions.

What Education and Certifications You Will Need

In all but exceptional cases, physical education teachers must be certified at the level and in the state in which they are teaching. Regardless of whether you are an elementary teacher in California or a high school teacher in New York, you will require certification. Some certification requirements are common across all

Meg Greiner

Physical education teacher at Independence Elementary School in Oregon

Photo courtesy of Meg Greiner.

Emphasizing how important it is to enjoy teaching children, Greiner says, "There are people who enter teaching and then discover that they don't really like kids. The most important quality is a love for children and desire to make a difference in their lives. It has to be part of your core. There is no option. For any teacher, there will always be trials and tribulations, so you have to truly believe in what you are doing. You have to love children; otherwise you will not make it further than your second year." Greiner was awarded the Disney Outstanding Specialist Teacher (2006) and named as National Association for Sport and Physical Education Elementary Teacher of the Year (2005).

states. For example, all 50 states may require that physical education teachers graduate from an accredited teacher education program at a college or university. Courses such as anatomy, curriculum, CPR and first-aid training, and technology may be requirements of these programs. Some state requirements, however, might be different. For example, some states require future teachers to pass basic skills tests in reading and math and may also mandate that they pass a state constitution test. Fortunately, most states have what is called *reciprocal agreements* so that a teacher certified in one state will be allowed to teach in another state. At most, teachers might have to pass a state exam or state constitution test in order to obtain the reciprocal certification. Many states also require teachers to pay a nominal fee every 5 to 10 years and enroll for continuing education in order to maintain certification.

Future Outlook

The outlook for physical education is quite positive. Concerns related to the obesity epidemic and the lack of physical activity opportunities for many children make school physical education all the more important. The recent "Let's Move" anti-obesity program spearheaded by First Lady Michelle Obama is but one of many national movements that emphasize the need for children to be active on a daily basis. For some students, their only opportunity to be active occurs during school. Physical education teachers who have dual certification in another subject matter area (e.g., math or science) and are willing to coach will be the most marketable. As physical activity is increasingly being recognized as a vital component of health, it will continue to become a prominent area in the school curriculum. Those physical education teachers who also engage as school physical activity leaders for both students and staff will be the most valued.

SPORT INSTRUCTOR

Many young people participate in school or nonschool sports and interact with instructors who have tremendous influence on their lives and involvement in sports and physical activity. As a child, did you have the opportunity to learn from or work with an experienced sport instructor who had a significant impact on your life? Perhaps you moved beyond the school or youth sport level and participated in university or college, or took lessons from a golf professional, swimming teacher, martial arts instructor, gymnastics coach, dance teacher, or rock climbing instructor who also influenced your career choices. Although sport instructors are much like coaches, typically sport instructors specialize in developing sport skills and competitive dispositions in the athlete. In essence, the sport instructor serves as a private mentor and gets the athlete ready to work with a coach. Sometimes the sport instructor *is* the athlete's coach.

Where You Will Work

Most sport instructors work in a variety of settings. It is estimated that over 200,000 individuals work in coaching and sport instructor positions in the United States. According to the U.S. Bureau of Labor Statistics, among those employed in wage and salaried positions, 52 percent hold jobs in public and private educational services, 13 percent work in recreational and commercial settings, and 16 percent are self-employed They work in school and nonschool settings. They also work in agencies such as the YMCA, the Boys' or Girls' Club, private clubs, specialized sport academies, and professional sport teams. Some work as employees of these agencies and some freelance or are self-employed and contracted with an agency or athlete. After reading this chapter, you might be interested in becoming employed as a private "tutor"—not to enhance the reading or writing skills of a child but to be a mentor in a specialized sport or even as a sport performance trainer for clients of varying ages. For example, you might elect to become a personal running coach for teenagers, a golf tutor for adults, or an exercise instructor for seniors in an assisted living facility.

Sport instructors have the flexibility of working in a variety of settings across the country and in various cities and locales within cities. They work in community settings (YMCAs, parks, and recreation departments), private clubs such as golf or tennis clubs, commercial settings (gymnastics studios, martial arts dojos or dojangs, dance studios, golf centers, and national centers such as Velocity Sports Performance, or local centers such as the Mayo Clinic Sports Performance Training Program), outdoor settings (mountain, river, or ocean for climbing, kayaking, scuba, or surfing), institutional settings (schools, colleges, and universities), and even in specialized sport academies.

Imagine how exciting it would be to work in the Sorenstam Golf Academy or one of the 15 IMG academies located primarily in Florida. The IMG academies serve over 12,000 clients at all levels (junior through professional) and across a variety of sports. Most certainly, if you possess specialized skills in teaching a sport offered in any of these settings, the potential for employment exists. In addition, if you achieve great success in any one of these settings, additional opportunities will emerge and you might be contracted to work with more elite or professional athletes. For example, many of the top golf instructors (David Leadbetter, Butch Harmon, Hank Haney) work with professional golfers. Opportunities might also exist for employment in a college or university campus recreation program with a need for a local expert to teach or coach a particular sport activity.

What You Will Do

Your job as a sport instructor will be to teach your students new skills or to refine their existing skills. You will also provide the knowledge base that addresses the strategic principles tied to the execution of a skill and the scientific knowledge (biomechanical, physiological, psychological, etc.) linked to the activity you teach. Motivating your clients is a key element of your instruction be it in the training facility where you are working or at a competitive event where your clients are competing. You will be responsible not only for instruction but held accountable for securing and maintaining facilities and equipment, overseeing the financial health of your "business," recruiting and retaining clients, advertising classes, and maintaining records. You will also be responsible for sustaining state-of-the-art knowledge and skill in your sport through your own continuing professional development.

Whom You Will Work With

The great thing about being a professional sport instructor is that your clientele crosses the lifespan. That is, depending on the sport, you might work with young children, teenagers, adolescents, or seniors. You may also elect to instruct novices, professionals, or both. For example, sport instruction in tennis, golf, dancing, figure skating, martial arts, and swimming, among others, can target either the young child or older adult. Although your learners are your primary clients, you will also have interactions with co-workers and others who support your enterprise (accountants, maintenance workers, medical practitioners, advertisers, administrators, and even parents).

What Personal Skills and Abilities You Will Need to Succeed

Beyond having advanced knowledge of the skill you are teaching and expertise in guiding the learning of clients, you must possess personal characteristics that promote success, including the following:

➤ **Tireless worker:** You will have to work some very unusual hours depending on the sport and your clientele.

➤ **Committed to professional development:** It will be important that you remain current in your sport and activity.

➤ **Disciplined:** It takes work to recruit clients, so you must be disciplined with your time and pay attention to this aspect of your job.

Master K. Young Chai

Owner and head instructor at Chai Tae Kwon Do (Lafayette, Indiana)

When asked, "What is the most satisfying to you as an instructor," Master Chai, who has achieved the status of 8th dan black belt, stated, "When they [students] are able to achieve what they want and when they become persons who are able to stand by themselves, that is very rewarding. When they start as white belts and can't do much and then they learn and are able to perform, that is very rewarding. The process can be (and often is) painstaking, but it's rewarding when you see growth at all levels."

Photo courtesy of Tom Templin.

When asked what advice he would give to those interested in becoming instructors within the martial arts, he advised, "Preparation; nothing but preparation is the key. Anyone who wants to get into martial arts instruction must know the martial art thoroughly. Secondly, they must know education—know what learning and motivation is; they must know what students want. It's not just one-sided; they have to know what the students want, what the parents want, and how this interacts with what the instructor wants and is prepared to teach." Chai's advice for would-be martial arts instructors rings just as true for those who want to teach other kinds of sports.

➤ **Expertise in assessment:** If you are to be helpful to your clients, you must have the ability to accurately assess their performance.

➤ **Reflective about your progress and open to midstream adjustments in your work:** You will need to continually reflect on your instruction and think about ways in which you most effectively teach your clientele. If something isn't working, you will need to adjust your mode of instruction.

➤ **Strong interpersonal skills:** To retain your clientele, you will need to sense their needs and be able to communicate effectively.

➤ **Track record of success throughout your career:** Your résumé is important; those who consider employing you want to know that you have current knowledge and skills and that you are someone they will enjoy working with.

What Education and Certifications You Will Need

Certification programs might or might not be available to enhance your role as a sport instructor. In some cases, a college degree will be sufficient. In other cases, professional endorsements from specific sport academies will be required. For example, Master Chai had to take many classes, practice for countless hours, and pass many skills tests before he attained his black belt status. Formal certification programs do exist for instructors of golf, tennis, soccer, gymnastics, fencing, and other sports. Various coaching programs also are available to help prepare youth coaches and others for working with children and adolescents in many sports. If you enroll in a sport instruction or coaching program, you will learn more about the sport or activity you are instructing and even how to teach that sport to different age groups.

Examples of organizations that provide sport instructors with varying levels of certification are the Ladies Professional Golf Association (LPGA), the U.S. Soccer Federation, and the Union of European Football Associations (UEFA). The LPGA Teaching and Club Professional Certification program aims to prepare golf instructors with a "high quality of professional skills" and features three levels of classification, culminating with a Class A credential.

The following associations provide sport instruction preparation, and some also offer certification programs:

➤ National Youth Sport Coaching Association

➤ American Coaching Education Program

➤ American Red Cross for certification to teach or coach swimming

➤ U.S. Soccer Federation

➤ National Coaches Association of America

➤ Professional Golfers' Association of America (currently there are over 28,000 certified professionals)

➤ Ladies Professional Golf Association

➤ United States Tennis Association

Future Outlook

With the increasing number of individuals who participate across the lifespan in various sports and physical activities, the future of sport instruction is bright. In fact, employment of coaches and sport instructors is expected to increase by 23 percent from 2008 to 2018. Well-prepared and highly qualified individuals who have instructional expertise will continue to have a role in our society. If you love sport, enjoy physical activity, and want to help others who are craving to learn how to participate in a particular sport, sport instruction is a great outlet for you. For some, sport instruction might supplement another job; for others, it will be a full-time job that can be relatively lucrative, depending on the sport or activity, nature of your clientele, extent of your knowledge, and level at which you are instructing.

COACH

If you enjoy working with others, love sports, and like to work in exciting environments, a career in coaching might be a great match for you. Competing and leading dozens of adolescents can have its benefits, perhaps the most important being you get to be involved in a sport you truly enjoy. Sport participation continues to grow at an astonishing rate, and the demand for coaches grows along with it. Coaching jobs for any age group, from preteen years and up, are attainable if you know the correct steps to get there.

Where You Will Work

One of the beauties of coaching is there are hundreds of settings where you can work. Getting your feet on the ground requires you to find a receptive sport organization and to volunteer. If you want to work with higher-level sport teams, you need to first put in your time at the lower ranks (unless you are one of those rare, amazing athletes recruited to coach at the more competitive level). Coaches typically work in three settings: community, institutional, and commercial.

➤ **Community settings:** In community settings coaches are responsible for the skill, moral, and social development of individuals they are coaching. Many positions are voluntary, but the excitement and psychological rewards and chance to influence young people are often far better than any monetary benefits. Most cities and towns have nonprofit service organizations that work toward meeting the social and civil values of the community. The Boys and Girls Club of America, YMCA, and YWCA are examples. Other nonprofit organizations such as Little League Baseball and Softball operate at the local, regional, district, national, and international levels and often rely entirely on volunteer coaches. In addition, most communities have sites where municipal recreational and sport-related activities occur for both youth and adults. Coaching within these settings can be casual to highly competitive, and many times you can coach and play at the same time.

➤ **Institutional settings** include local schools, colleges, and universities. Most private and public schools offer extracurricular athletic programs, and becoming a teacher or administrator is the surest way of acquiring a coaching job. According to the Bureau of Labor Statistics, in May of 2008 the average sport coach at the high school and middle-school level will make a stipend between $2,500 and $10,000 (U.S.) for the season, but sports such as football and basketball can bring much higher stipends depending on the revenue or recognition they bring to the school. If you are privileged enough to coach at the college or university level, you will have to answer to those who hold strong allegiances to their teams. Coaching at this level can be a high-pressured job that is not for everyone. It requires the highest level of expertise and winning results. The salary, however, is very lucrative. An article from the January 10, 2009, *USA Today* reported that for college football in 2009, "3 coaches received at least $4 million, 9 received at least $3 million, 25 received at least $2 million, and 56 pulled in at least $1 million." This wage is quite different from that of the average college football coach at a small state university, who typically makes between $50,000 and $250,000.

➤ **Commercial settings:** The most glorified of all coaching jobs is working as a coach of a professional team. Although you would live a financially comfortable life and travel from one sport arena to another, the pressure to win is extremely high. Obtaining a position at this level is difficult and generally requires experience as an athlete, strong knowledge of the sport, and considerable coaching experience. Coaching salaries in the "for profit" arena depend on revenue generated from fan attendance, type of sport, and acquired success. At the highest level, coaches make in excess of $1 million annually. Commercial settings include large arenas, stadiums, and practice facilities of professional teams. They also might include sports and country clubs that focus on golf, tennis, swimming, basketball, and soccer. Coaching at the commercial level requires an extremely high level of expertise.

What You Will Do

The coach's primary responsibilities are to plan, organize, and conduct practice sessions and to guide the team (or individuals) during competition. There is, however, a great deal more to coaching than just planning and organizing practices. According to the occupational information network O*NET OnLine, the following skills are essential:

➤ **Management:** Distribute and organize equipment; keep statistics and records; organize assistant staff and delegate responsibilities; scout opposing teams and future recruits; and file athlete reports.

➤ **Leadership:** Direct practice sessions; provide training direction and motivation; plan strategies and adjust techniques; develop game strategies; instruct individuals or groups about sport rules, game strategies, performance principles, and skill development; and plan and direct physical conditioning programs.

➤ **Motivation:** Provide encouragement; build motivational techniques into practices and games; give leadership responsibilities to athletes; provide developmentally appropriate tasks; instill goal settings; and provide experiences for character building and team building.

➤ **Role modeling:** Establish consistency in expectations and standards of conduct and model them; demonstrate important values and character traits such as dependability, integrity, cooperation, tolerance, good sporting behavior, effort, achievement, initiative, leadership, flexibility, persistence, cooperation, and concern for others.

➤ **Provide for safety:** Ensure that the natural environment and equipment are set up for the safest possible scenario at all times; plan and strategize beforehand for safety during practice and games; and always maintain heightened awareness of potential danger to participants and fans in any given situation.

Unlike physical education teachers and sport instructors, who spend the majority of their time in instructional roles, coaches at higher levels tend to spend much time engaged in the responsibilities of scheduling and recruiting. Compare the duties of sport instructors and coaches in figure 4.1.

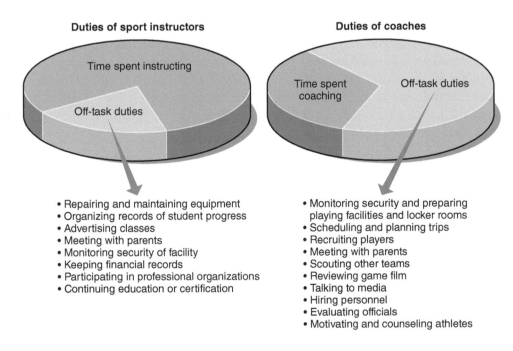

Figure 4.1   Duties of sport instructors and coaches.

Adapted, by permission, from S. Hoffman, 2009, Careers in coaching and sport instruction. In *Introduction to kinesiology*, 3rd ed., edited by S.J. Hoffman. (Champaign, IL: Human Kinetics), 444. Based on the study of G.M. DeMarco 1999.

For most youth sport and school coaches, coaching is a part-time endeavor. Following their day jobs as teachers, they fulfill the duties of their coaching job in the evening. The long days only last a short season, and then you spend the rest of the year waiting excitedly for your coaching season to return. The length of your season depends on the level and the sport, with many elite teams competing year-round. On average, most youth sport seasons last less than two months. High school and middle-school sports usually go a little longer, particularly if there is postseason play. When you have gained enough experience, you might be able to move up to the college level, where you will likely train and work with your athletes on a full-day schedule for the entire year.

Whom You Will Work With

As a coach, you are almost guaranteed to work with youth at some point in your coaching career. According to the National Council of Youth Sports, over 52 million youths between the ages of 6 and 18 participate in sport in the United States. A survey by the Sporting Goods Manufacturers Association in January 2009 indicated that youth basketball was the number one sport in the United States, with 26.2 million participants. Baseball was second with 15 million, and soccer third with 14.2 million. Newer sports are generating increasing interest—lacrosse brings in over 1.1 million participants. Sports such as paintball and cheerleading had dramatic increases as well as snowboarding, skateboarding, and mountain biking.

Coaches for adult populations are not nearly in as much demand as those for adolescents. The majority of the adult coaching positions include college-level athletics where the athletes' age range is from 19 to 24. Leisure activities such as walking, jogging, bicycle riding, hiking, swimming, aerobic fitness, yoga, weight training, billiards, motor-boating, fishing, and target shooting are the most popular activities in various regions of the United States for those over the age of 18, but there are still many adults who love sport and competition. The most popular adult sports in which you might find coaching opportunities in the U.S. are softball, basketball, and bowling, along with individual sports such as tennis and golf.

What Personal Skills and Abilities You Will Need to Succeed

Whether you elect coaching as a career because of your own involvement in sport or because you enjoy working with athletes, coaching requires more than simply knowing the game or sport. Personal skills are critical for becoming a respected coach. Coaches with charisma and who show great confidence and poise, and those who inspire athletes to achieve high levels of success both personally and in the game, are the coaches considered most successful. Skills and abilities that O*NET lists as most critical for coaches include the following:

➤ **Confidence and poise:** Coaches must be able to take charge and handle criticism.

➤ **Dependability:** This characteristic is critical because athletes and parents will rely on you to be consistently responsible.

➤ **Honesty, integrity, and inspiration:** It is important that coaches demonstrate upstanding personal behavior and uphold the values of the community, school, or commercial organization.

➤ **Perseverance and dedication:** Coaches must learn to overcome obstacles and demonstrate loyalty to their organization and athletes.

➤ **Flexibility and cooperation:** Coaches must be responsive to the needs of others. Flexibility and cooperation are often necessary.

➤ **Sensitivity and perspective:** Coaches are responsible for attending to the needs and feelings of athletes, parents, and the organization.

➤ **Sport training:** Coaches must have strong knowledge of the sport they are coaching and be skilled at conveying that knowledge to their athletes.

➤ **Psychosocial knowledge:** An understanding of dynamics of human behavior and performance is necessary for coaches at all levels.

➤ **Communication:** The abilities to listen and to speak effectively are important for success in coaching.

➤ **Organization:** The skill of managing all activities within the organization is required of all coaches.

What Education and Certifications You Will Need

Most coaches are trained in their sport by having played it at some level. Regardless of how you obtain exposure to a sport, it is essential to have a firm understanding of the knowledge of the sport's rules, regulations, and strategies. This knowledge base can come in many ways.

➤ **Development of coaching experience:** The development of your coaching career—from playing the sport as an athlete, to volunteer coaching, to working as an assistant coach—is crucial to obtaining higher level coaching jobs. Obtaining additional training outside of coaching that includes earning certifications, attending sports camps, participating in the sport, or obtaining a degree in one of the areas of kinesiology highlighted in this book is also critical to moving up the ranks more quickly.

➤ **Certification and licensure:** The requirements for certification and licensure vary by sport, level, and setting. Although coaches in youth sport programs tend not to be certified, the ASEP Professional Coaches Education Program and the National Youth Sport Coaching Association offer certification programs, as do other associations that are specific to particular sports. Within civic organizations, certification requirements vary by level of competition. At the middle-school and high school levels, coaches usually need to meet state requirements for certification. Most coaching positions in institutional settings require first-aid and CPR certification and criminal background checks. Several nonprofit sporting organiza-

Anita Boeck

2009 National High School Coach of the Year for volleyball

Successful coaching goes beyond helping one's clientele to acquire skills and knowledge about a particular sport, according to Coach Boeck. It also involves team building. She states, "In all of my years of coaching, the aspect I have enjoyed the most is taking a group of girls who have different interests, per-

© Anita Barrios

sonalities, strengths, weaknesses, and goals (which can sometimes lead to conflict) and watching them bond until they truly are a *team* in every sense of the word."

tions have certification programs but often require training before you can begin coaching in their programs. College-level coaching sometimes requires certification requirements and usually requires a college degree unless you have been an elite athlete in the sport.

Future Outlook

Many youth and school sports have shown increased participation over the past few years. This increase is consistent with previous years as youth sport and school sport have both had tremendous growth over the past decade. Although opportunities at the college, university, and professional levels are very limited, there is and will continue to be a need for coaches at the youth and school levels. The earlier you start, the faster you will move up the coaching ranks. According to the Bureau of Labor Statistics there is a projected need for 99,200 additional employees above the current number of coaches over the next few years. In 2008, 226,000 coaches were employed at a median wage of $28,340 (U.S.). The projected demand is much faster than average (20 percent or higher), owing to increased attention being given to physical activity as a way of controlling the obesity epidemic among children. Population growth, advancement of age and demand for senior activities, increased female interest in sports, and coaching attrition caused by retirement will add to the need.

SPORTS OFFICIAL

According to the National Sports Officiating Organization, over 300,000 men and women serve as sports officials. Many more will be needed because sports officiating continues to be a rapidly growing field. Did you love playing recreational and competitive sports as a child? Would you enjoy an active and challenging profession?

If your answers are yes, and if you value staying connected to athletics, a career in sports officiating is worth considering.

Where You Will Work

Officials work in many environments. They officiate in minimally maintained neighborhood parks and in small, stuffy gyms. They also officiate games within beautiful, multimillion dollar facilities in which the contests are the focus of national and international media. Here are a few other settings in which you could work as a sports official:

➤ **Community and recreation leagues:** This includes working for a park district as an official for any number of team or individual sports. Officials are in demand, for example, for youth soccer, a women's volleyball league geared toward a 40+ age group, advanced Tae Kwan Do competitions, and 3-on-3 summer basketball tournaments. Many sport clubs and intramural programs also hire officials.

➤ **Elementary, middle, and high school:** While mastering the rules and officiating procedures for a particular sport or two, you might start off volunteering as an official for elementary school athletic events. When you feel ready, you can move up the ranks to middle and high school games.

➤ **College and university:** After logging some experience at the lower levels and earning the appropriate credentials, some officials seek employment in the college or university ranks, possibly starting off at the junior college level before moving up to division III, II, and I.

➤ **Professional:** Only a select few officials make it to the professional ranks to officiate in such high-profile leagues as the NFL, NBA, WNBA, NHL, or MLB. The route to the top might or might not require experience at each of the lower levels of officiating; above all, success requires an extraordinarily high level of skill.

Sports officiating conditions vary from situation to situation, but one thing is certain: officiating is not for the faint of heart. Listed below are working conditions of officials; whether you perceive them as positive or negative will tell you a lot about whether this career might be for you.

➤ **Travel:** Generally speaking, as you move up the ladder of sports officiating (i.e., from community or recreation, to elementary, middle, and high school, to college, and finally to professional), travel demands increase. Officials for Pee Wee football travel little. High school football officials travel to schools in the region. College football officials often travel across the country. Professional football officials spend many nights in hotels during the season.

➤ **Irregular hours:** More often than not, athletic contests are played in the late afternoon and evening; sometimes they are played on weekends and even holidays.

➤ **Weather:** Officials for outdoor sports often must endure unfavorable weather conditions. Running up and down a lacrosse field with snow on the ground doesn't appeal to everyone. On the other hand, working outside on a balmy, sunny day is a treat for most people.

➤ **Stress:** Sports officials must deal with the pressure of making split-second decisions. Sometimes they bear the brunt of verbal abuse from players, coaches, and fans who disagree with their decisions. In extreme cases, officials have been physically attacked by passionate, irrational sports zealots.

➤ **Money:** Salary scales for sports officials vary depending on the sport and the level at which you work and whether or not officiating is a full-time occupation. According to the U.S. Department of Labor, officials in the middle 50 percent range of salaries earn between $17,410 and $33,150 (U.S.). Those in the lower range of salaries are likely to be officials working within community, recreation, and school leagues, whereas those in the middle range are likely to be those working for college and university athletic conferences or minor league professional sports. Officials who work for major professional leagues earn much more; major league baseball umpires, for example, earn between $100,000 to $300,000 per year with a $357 per diem for hotels and meals. Minor league officials can expect to earn between $1,800 to $3,400 per month. NFL officials earn between $2,000 and $7,000 per game; NHL officials earn an average of $140,000, and NBA officials earn $130,000 on average.

What You Will Do

Officials oversee athletic events, maintaining order by calling rule violations and imposing penalties as established by the rules and regulations of the sport. Depending on the sport, officials work individually or as part of a team. Officials at high school and higher levels usually are assigned games and schedules by a central office. Usually one official is assigned primary responsibility for the officiating squad. At upper-level university and professional levels, officials usually arrive the day before the contest to prepare. Officials working at high school through the professional ranks are evaluated regularly and assigned ratings. These ratings determine which games they will work.

Whom You Will Work With

Officials must collaborate and cooperate with many people. With few exceptions, officials must learn to work in tandem with others. These include other officials, athletic directors, coaches, players, and those working in the league office who evaluate and assign officials. Usually each of these parties has its own agenda, its own expectations of the official, and its own vested interest. Although officials don't actually work with spectators, when crowd behavior adversely affects a contest it usually falls to officials to find a solution.

What Personal Skills and Abilities You Will Need to Succeed

It seems unlikely that anyone would want to be an official without having passion for a sport, or perhaps many sports. That said, in order to pave a path of success on your journey to become a sports official, some skills and abilities are required.

➤ **Fitness:** Most sports require that you move up and down a court or field to get the best view of the action. This requires cardiovascular and muscular endurance.

➤ **Knowledge of the game:** Understanding the game's rules, regulations, and penalties, including how to rule on rare occurrences, is essential. Knowing how to signal violations and other decisions to teams, coaches, and crowds is also important. Officials at the higher levels of a sport are usually required to attend continuing education sessions to stay abreast of updates on the rules.

➤ **Resilience:** The pressure of making difficult calls, the task of ignoring the nasty commentary of unruly fans, and the sometimes unpleasant reality of handling the negative attitudes of coaches and players requires strength of spirit.

What Education and Certifications You Will Need

The type of education and training you will need for officiating depends heavily on the sport and level at which you want to work. The best advice for those seeking to get a foot in the door by working for community sport organizations is to contact the organization directly, be it the local recreation department, YMCA, or YWCA. Information is also available through the National Federation of State High School Associations. Other organizations include the National Association of Sports Officials, and *Referee* magazine. A degree in kinesiology is not a requirement for sports officiating, but having the broad background of information about sports and exercise that typically is taught in kinesiology departments will surely be an advantage. See table 4.1 for the training required for different levels of baseball officiating.

Future Outlook

The future of sports officiating looks bright. It has been projected that jobs associated with athletics will grow faster than the average for all occupations. According to the Bureau of Labor Statistics, the number of sports officials is expected to rise by 10 percent from 2008 to 2018.

Table 4.1 Baseball Officiating Requirements by Level

Community, recreation, & elementary school leagues	High school leagues	College leagues	Minor leagues	Major leagues
• Training course • Knowledge exam	• Register with overseeing state agency • Knowledge exam	• Certified by an officiating school • Evaluated during probationary period • Residence in or near conference boundaries • Several years of experience officiating at the high school or community college level	• Umpire training school	• 7 to 10 years of experience at the minor league level before being considered

Adapted from the Bureau of Labor Statistics 2008. Available: www.bls.gov/oco/ocos251.htm#training

Gary Crull

**NCAA division I
college football official**

© Human Kinetics

In addition to having a love for the sport, officials must focus on preparation, communication, and comportment. "Preparation is important," says Crull, because "the game you are working on any given day is the most important game in the country for the athletes on that field. It doesn't matter what level you are working, if you aren't ready, you are cheating the athletes, coaches, and the sport." Communication is important because "highly emotional situations can often be handled by listening, and offering an explanation. All interactions should be professional, friendly, respectful, and brief." Finally, he stresses the importance of comportment—the official's behavior and manner on the field. "You are often judged by coaches, athletes, and spectators before the game even starts. Present yourself with the utmost professionalism from the time you arrive at a game site until you leave. If you take pride in the way you look and work a contest, it sends a message. There are no shortcuts to success in officiating. If you hustle, are decisive, poised, and consistent you will send a message that you care about your job and approach it as a professional."

SPORT PSYCHOLOGIST

Sport psychology is the study and application of psychological factors that influence behavior and performance in sport, exercise, and physical activity. Although sport psychology has existed for nearly 100 years, it is only in the last few decades that increasing numbers of coaches and athletes have come to recognize that performance success is not the result only of technical and physical skill but finely honed psychological skills as well. Sport psychologists work with athletes on motivation and performance skills and help them deal with the intense pressures often associated with high-level athletics. Professional golfers have long looked to sport psychologists to help prepare them for the rigors of competing in the PGA or LPGA. Some professional sport teams and university athletic departments hire sport psychologists (often called mental skills consultants) to work with their teams and individual athletes. Sport psychology has also become an integral element in the preparation of Olympic athletes.

Sport psychology is not for elite athletes only. The mental game is just as important in youth sports as in professional leagues. Many sport psychologists work with youth programs and young athletes; others develop programs and resources for coaches. Also, *sport* in sport psychology goes beyond competitive athletics to include exercise and physical activity in clinical rehabilitation settings. Some sport psychologists consult with clients in fitness centers and sports medicine clinics to help them stick to their exercise programs.

Where You Will Work

Sport psychologists work in many venues and at many levels. Here are a few you might find interesting:

➤ **College athletics:** After acquiring enough education and experience, some sport psychologists work as consultants for college or university teams and athletes (usually not on a full-time basis).

➤ **Professional/national sport programs:** Psychological preparation is critically important at the elite levels of competition. Some professional teams hire full-time or part-time psychological consultants. These jobs are very difficult to obtain—you have to prove yourself as being one of the best.

➤ **Private practice:** Increasing numbers of sport psychologists work in private practice and consult with teams or individuals. These consultants are often licensed psychologists or professional counselors, and sport psychology is only part of their professional practice.

➤ **University professor or researcher:** Since the late 1960s, sport psychology has been an important part of the curriculum for students enrolled in undergraduate kinesiology programs. Professors specializing in sport and exercise psychology work in these departments teaching and conducting research on the psychological parameters of sport and exercise behavior.

A few sport psychologists earn six-figure salaries working as consultants for professional athletes. Most however earn substantially less, depending on their reputations and reported success. Academic sport psychologists work at the collegiate level and can expect to earn the average salary for university faculty positions, which typically starts around $50,000 (U.S.) and ranges into six figures depending on rank and institution.

What You Will Do

If you were to compare a sports contest to a theatrical production, a sport psychologist would be one of the key members of the backstage crew. If you weren't there behind the stage, the play would still go on, but it wouldn't operate efficiently or effectively. The sport psychologist's role varies depending on the position and setting in which he or she works. Sport psychologists might work with a team, helping players develop anxiety-management techniques; concentration

Diane Gill, PhD

Professor of sport and exercise psychology at the University of North Carolina at Greensboro

"Professional roles in sport psychology are often listed as research, teaching, and consulting, and I add advocacy. Regardless of the primary career, all sport psychology professionals play all roles and need each key quality. All sport psychology professionals must be scholars who engage in systematic problem solving and evidence-based practice. As teachers they focus on how their students, clients, colleagues, and the general public learn about sport psychology. Successful professionals also draw on experiential knowledge and blend science and art in consulting activities. And, in my view, all sport psychology professionals must be advocates for sport psychology in the public interest, using sport psychology to promote physical activity for the health and well-being of all."

Photo courtesy of Diane Gill.

strategies; and goal-setting, communication, team–building, and imagery skills. Sport psychologists working at the collegiate level perform roles in addition to those already mentioned. For example, a sport psychologist working with an athletic program might also act as advising coordinator and career counselor. A sport psychologist on a college faculty might teach classes in sport psychology and other kinesiology areas, and also conduct research on sport and exercise psychology.

Whom You Will Work With

Sport psychologists consulting on mental skills work directly with athletes who are the beneficiaries of their services. They interact with coaches, athletic administrators, and team owners as well, but their primary personal and professional obligation is to the athletes they are trying to help. Sport psychologists working in fitness or sports medicine settings work directly with clients and might also work with other professionals in that setting on psychological skills and strategies. Injured athletes or persons with disabilities or chronic conditions might require counseling or clinical services beyond the expertise of the sport psychologist. Sport psychologists with clinical training and certifications might work in collaboration with sports medicine professionals and licensed psychologists.

What Personal Skills and Abilities You Will Need to Succeed

As a sport psychologist, you must be interested in people. Along with a sound foundation in sport psychology knowledge, you should be caring, compassionate, service oriented and committed to the overall development of sport participants. Effective communication skills, patience, and sensitivity are musts.

What Education and Certifications You Will Need

Sport psychologists must recognize their limitations and deliver services only within the boundaries of their competence. High-level consulting, conducting research, or teaching at the college level generally requires a PhD. Although many kinesiology programs offer sport psychology courses, most do not offer a sport psychology degree for undergraduate students. The Association for Applied Sport Psychology suggests pursuing a double major in psychology and kinesiology at the undergraduate level, or obtaining a degree in one of the disciplines and a minor in the other. Volunteering to work with a faculty member on a research project related to the psychology of sport or exercise is also recommended, as is gaining experience through working as a coach or counselor.

The Association for Applied Sport Psychology (AASP) offers certification and resources for professionals in the field. Certification as an AASP consultant allows you to be registered with the United States Olympic Committee Sport Psychology Registry and to work with Olympic athletes and national teams. Professional practice in clinical sport psychology requires appropriate training and licensing in clinical psychology or counseling.

Future Outlook

The future looks hopeful for those choosing careers in sport psychology. The demand for mental skills training has increased with sport participation at all levels. Sport psychology is no longer reserved for elite athletes. Many youth and recreational athletes, and the professionals who work with them, are interested in these benefits. Learning how to concentrate, focus, increase motivation, and control emotion is desirable to anyone looking for that extra competitive edge or a path to greater health and fitness.

The authors wish to thank Diane Gill and Shirl Hoffman for their significant contributions to the sport psychology section of this chapter.

Chapter 5

Careers in Sport Marketing and Management

Marlene A. Dixon

S port management is an exciting academic and career field that has boomed over the past 20 years. Sport economist Dan Mahoney and his colleagues have estimated that the sport industry has grown to over a $152 billion (U.S.) industry employing about 800,000 people throughout the United States. Further, according to major business indexes such as Dun and Bradstreet and Hoovers, the professional sport team industry in the United States alone is composed of over 800 organizations, generating over $16 billion (U.S.) annually. The sport manager job, popularized by the film *Jerry McGuire,* led many people to think of sport managers as sport agents. Others think of sport managers as recreational sport coaches or administrators. The field is much broader, however, encompassing such careers as athletic directors, sport journalists, public relations and media specialists, marketers, facility operators, and event specialists. Have you dreamed of running an advertising campaign for Adidas, managing the athletic department at Notre Dame, or helping organize the Olympics? If yes, then sport management might be the career for you.

SPORT ADMINISTRATOR

Some of the most popular and intriguing careers in the sport industry are in sport administration. Such careers include general manager (GM) of a professional team, athletic director at the high school or college level, or director of a community's youth sport programs.

Where You Will Work

A sport administrator might work in professional sport as the general manager of a sport franchise. In this setting, the manager usually works out of the team's main office and travels with the team to most of their away games. A GM of a professional franchise, such as in the NFL, NBA, or MLB, would expect to make at least $200,000 (U.S.) annually and perhaps up to more than $1 million depending on the team and the manager's experience. College athletic directors work at their college or university, which is often an attractive setting that allows the director to be around young, bright people, and often affords travel opportunities with the team and for conference, NCAA, or NAIA meetings. Salaries range from $50,000 to over $500,000 depending on the size of the institution, the scope of the athletic program, and the conference in which the school's team competes. Most college athletic directors truly enjoy the sport experience and claim that a favorite perk of the job is attending many great sporting events.

High school athletic directors usually work on the campus of their high school, but sometimes they work in the district's main administrative central office or even in an athletic administration central office. High school athletic directors might be campus coordinators of activities (which usually also involves a coaching position or other administrative position), or they might be responsible for the athletic activities for an entire school district. The high school administrator is generally available at most home athletic events; most of them work nights and weekends and must do some traveling in their jobs. Most work well beyond a 40-hour work week. Some administrators (especially at the high school level) also have coaching duties, which can add to their work demands. This work environment can be especially difficult for maintaining a balance in work and personal life. Salaries for high school athletic administrators range from $50,000 to just over $100,000, depending on the scope of the job and size of the school district.

What You Will Do

Sport administrators are responsible for personnel decisions regarding coaches, athletes, and support staff such as trainers, marketing staff, and equipment managers. Sport administrators hire, train, oversee, evaluate, transfer, trade, and promote employees. Typically, they also supervise financial operations, including fund-raising and financial development, as well as overseeing the annual budget and day-to-day spending. Sport administrators are responsible for coordinating the activities of teams and athletic departments and for overseeing all facilities and equipment. They are ultimately responsible for care and maintenance of facilities and usually are intimately involved with the planning and construction of new facilities. Although the stresses on sport administrators have increased over the past 20 years, most find the jobs very rewarding personally and professionally. They enjoy the sport atmosphere and the opportunity to help young people achieve their dreams and goals.

Whom You Will Work With

One of the most interesting and challenging aspects of the sport administrator position is working with a wide variety of people. A general manager of an NFL franchise, for example, works with the owner of the franchise as well as with coaches, athletes, trainers, and support personnel within the organization. The GM also works with venue managers and field maintenance personnel (including turf management, food and concession sales, etc.) as well as with other NFL GMs to coordinate schedules, player drafts, and other related business. Most GMs work with city managers and other VIPS in the city to promote the franchise and develop good community relations. Similarly, college or high school athletic directors would work with their own staff and athletes as well as with the college's or high school's main administrators, teachers, parents, and community members.

What Personal Skills and Abilities You Will Need to Succeed

Sport administrators need a blend of personal skills and abilities to succeed in their careers. First and foremost, they need people skills. They need to be able to negotiate successfully with other constituents, to evaluate talent, to discuss training and development needs, to handle disagreements among staff, and to motivate their employees to perform their best. Managers also need leadership skills in order to set a vision for the organization, and to help everyone stay focused on accomplishing the objectives that lead to the realization of this vision. An organization's vision often involves winning games, but it might also include achieving financial viability or efficiency and developing personnel. The general manager and athletic director also require financial and budgeting skills to be successful along with a general knowledge of contracts and legal issues surrounding personnel, facilities, liability, and governing bodies. This knowledge helps the sport administrator make wise decisions in the daily management of the organization and avoid costly public relations and legal mishaps.

What Education and Certifications You Will Need

No official certifications are required for employment as a sport administrator. In the past, many sport administrators have come to their positions from coaching backgrounds. They coached for a number of years and then moved to administrative positions as they gained experience or wanted a career shift. This career path is still somewhat typical in a high school setting, where an aspiring athletic director would first need to obtain a teaching or coaching degree or certificate, and then an advanced degree in sport management or educational administration.

In college and professional sports, however, it is less common for sport administrators to move from the coaching ranks into sport administration. Owing to the increasing emphasis being placed on sports as a commercial enterprise, most sport administrators at these levels have acquired education and experience in marketing, accounting, personnel management, finance, and event design and management as well as grounding in the social, cultural, and ethical aspects of sport. Aspiring athletic administrators often seek positions that will prepare them in each facet of athletic administration. A broad background in all facets of administration better prepares them to compete for the top jobs in the country. The best place to launch your career in athletic administration is at the undergraduate level. Follow this up with advanced graduate work to add to your marketability. According to the North American Society for Sport Management (NASSM), over 286 universities in the United States offer an accredited undergraduate and/or graduate-level degree in sport management.

Future Outlook

Although competition for these positions remains high, the employment prospects for administration careers is fairly bright. According to the U.S. Department of Labor (USDL), employment in the educational, nonprofit sector for administrators is expected to grow by about 8 percent between 2008 and 2018. This is the average growth expected for all occupations. With an anticipated increase in the rate of retirement of current administrators, the prospects for attaining these positions is greater than in the recent past. The Bureau of Labor points to the western and southern parts of the United States as regions likely to experience the fastest growth. Prospects are less encouraging for the Northeast and Midwest.

Within the private sector, the USDL expects only small growth in employment as well as keen competition for top-level managers in the sport industry. However, because these positions are essential to organizations, well-qualified applicants will still be able to find positions relative to the growth in the industry. Thus, as the sport industry continues to grow, positions in management will continue to be available. These positions are likely to be filled by people both within the sport industry and from general business professions. Successful athletic administrators at any level will need excellent training, social networking, and commitment to the profession in order to succeed.

SPORT MARKETER

Professionals working in sport marketing create advertising and promotion campaigns that attract participants, fans, and sponsors to a sport or team. Sport marketers try to understand and estimate consumer demand for their product or service, and then deliver it in such a way that customers will be satisfied and want to repeat the experience.

Where You Will Work

Sport marketers might work for a professional team such as the Denver Broncos or Boston Red Sox, for a full-service management and marketing organization such as International Management Group (IMG), or for a participant sport organization such as a YMCA, or for a college or university. In each case, the job of sport marketer is one of the most attractive and widely available career tracks in sport. All sport organizations want to attract fans and sponsors because they bring revenue to the organization; thus, sport organizations always need great marketers.

The daily responsibilities and work conditions within sport marketing tend to vary by season. Consider the job of marketing manager at the Houston Texans (see Daniel Velasco's profile). In the off-season, the marketing staff works in the office 9 to 5 conducting evaluations and budget reviews and planning for the upcoming season. On at least two weekends per month, the marketers might also be out in the local community hosting fan and youth events. As the season nears, the marketing staff will host events for the official NFL draft as well as promote season ticket sales. During the playing season, sport marketers work very long hours planning and carrying out promotions and campaigns on nearly every day of the week, including game day. This work might be done in the office, in the community, or at the stadium. The work is fun and energetic, but it is not unusual for a sport marketer to work 70 to 80 hours per week during the season, including many nights and both weekend days. According to salary.com, experienced sport marketers for a professional team or university make between $60,000 and $90,000 (U.S.); new employees' salaries often start around $40,000. Sport marketers in a full-service marketing firm can make anywhere from $60,000 to over $400,000 depending on their clients and their salary structure (base vs. commission).

Daniel Velasco

Marketing manager for the Houston Texans NFL franchise

Often a penchant for innovation is what sets one sport marketer above another. With four years of experience in his current position, Velasco says the following about succeeding in a sport marketing career: "Always be open-minded and willing to work hard at whatever you do. In addition, good communication skills and the ability to work with lots of different people can make you successful in sport marketing. I love what I do, so it usually doesn't feel like a job."

Photo courtesy of Daniel Velasco.

What You Will Do

Sport marketers estimate the demand for their team or organization's product and services and then create advertising, promotions, and sales opportunities that will meet that demand. Sport consumers—the targets of the sport marketer's efforts—include actual participants (e.g., golf club members, youth soccer players, adult recreation league participants), sport fans (e.g., fans who attend games, watch games on television, purchase season tickets, or purchase merchandise), and sport sponsors (i.e., companies who pay money to have their product associated with an athlete or team). Depending on the job, a sport marketer might be involved in marketing to any or all of these groups.

Consider a marketing director for a PGA event. This individual is responsible first and foremost for marketing the event to the golfers themselves—convincing them of the benefits and opportunities of playing in this event. The PGA sport marketer is also responsible for attracting spectators to the event—because event tickets, concessions, and merchandise are important sources of revenue. Finally, the marketer is responsible for attracting sponsors and selling them on the benefits of being associated with the event, which include television exposure, an attractive site for hosting clients, and other advertising opportunities. (For example, last year Wells Fargo paid about $7 million to be the title sponsor of the Quail Hollow Championship in Charlotte, North Carolina.) The marketer must work with all three consumer groups in mind and develop plans for each according to their needs and wants.

Sport marketers employed by a college or university athletic department are responsible for attracting fans and sponsors and for promoting sporting events on campus. Another variety of marketing involves agents who secure lucrative endorsements and sponsorships for star athletes. This is a highly specialized form of marketing that often requires a law degree and expertise in negotiation. Whereas jobs are relatively plentiful in sport marketing, launching a career as a sport agent is extraordinarily difficult.

Jobs in sport marketing can be really fun. Designing promotions and marketing tools ranging from player and mascot appearances, to throwing t-shirts out of a blaster, to giving away bobblehead dolls and other free stuff. Some marketers claim that minor league baseball and hockey have the most creative and crazy marketing promotions, including a Salute to Indoor Plumbing and a World's Largest Tighty-Whitey Race by the West Virginia Power and a Mustache Growing Contest by the Vero Beach Devil Rays. Thus, although the hours are long, most sport marketers really enjoy what they do.

Whom You Will Work With

In college and professional team marketing, sport marketers work with the directors of advertising and branding, the sponsors themselves, the television and radio producers, the events staff, and sometimes marketing research specialty firms to create and coordinate their efforts. Marketers must make sure their ideas are consistent in message and quality with those of their organization, and that necessary resources are available to conduct the events and promotions that they want to offer. For example, if the Chicago Cubs want to have a Kerry Wood Bobblehead Night, they must make sure that the marketing and target audience are correct, that they have a sponsor to pay for the bobbleheads and the personnel to give them out, and that the night of the promotion is coordinated and promoted through television and radio.

In agency marketing, sport marketers (agents) work with athletes and companies to create sponsor partnerships. They also work with companies to create advertising and promotions. In addition, an agent might work with athletes' teams to coordinate appearances and other obligations through sponsorships.

What Personal Skills and Abilities You Will Need to Succeed

As you can see, sport marketers work with many people both out in front with the product or service and behind the scenes creating and coordinating the final product or event. This can be exciting, but it requires great communication skills and flexibility. Marketers must be able to think on their feet and problem-solve during events and promotions, especially when schedule, personnel, and sometimes even the nature of the event itself require adjustments. Marketers should be creative and energetic, open-minded, and willing to try new things.

What Education and Certifications You Will Need

Employers prefer individuals with a bachelor's or master's degree in sport management or general management with an emphasis or specialization in marketing. Within sport management, a specialization in sport marketing is useful because it provides training in the distinct consumer elements of sport (as opposed to generalized marketing and management). Courses such as sport marketing, marketing research, consumer behavior, sales and promotions, sport law (especially contract law), communications, and public relations can give sport marketers a foundation for meeting the challenges in this occupation. In addition, near the end of their schooling, most aspiring sport marketers complete an internship in a related field, which provides practical experience and builds their employment networks.

Future Outlook

According to the U.S. Department of Labor, jobs in general marketing management are expected to grow by 13 percent by 2018. Marketing job growth will continue because of the competition for consumers. As more products and services, both in North America and globally, flood the market, clever sport marketers using innovative techniques will be needed to make a product or service stand out from the crowd. Although growth in the field is expected, so is intense competition, because jobs in marketing (especially sport marketing) are highly desirable. Because sport marketers generate revenue for their organizations, those who perform well tend to be retained or promoted to higher levels within the organizations.

MEDIA AND PUBLIC RELATIONS

Another popular sport management career is a media or public relations (PR) specialist. A media or PR specialist is in charge of communicating with the public about the team or sport organization, trying to generate fan and media interest and awareness about the team and individual athletes, coaches, and other personnel.

Where You Will Work

People in this career track might work for a firm that handles only media relations, yet most teams and sport organizations have their media and PR personnel in-house. Thus, if you pursue this career with success you will most likely work for a university or a professional sport team. Media and PR specialists work in exciting, fast-paced environments. They often travel with the team so that they can write up stories about the team and keep abreast of all the latest developments. During the playing season, they work many nights and weekends, often staying up late to communicate with the public and the media about game results and to relay relevant stories about the day's happenings. In the off-season, they work more regular hours except when nearing deadlines for such materials as articles or media guides or when encountering a public relations crisis such as an athlete's arrest.

Like other occupations in sport, most media and PR specialists like their working conditions. They enjoy being in a college or professional organization, and they like being around and writing about sport. Media and PR specialists can expect to make $50,000 to $80,000 (U.S.) depending on the type of firm they work for and their level of experience.

What You Will Do

To develop and maintain good relations with fans and community and to inform them of events and happenings involving the team, media and PR personnel often write regular press releases as well as web-based materials such as blogs and online newsletters. Media and PR staff also plan and conduct press conferences to release information or alert the media to actions, accomplishments, or changes in the club. Media and PR staff help their organization build goodwill and communications with the public. They can do this through promoting or calling attention to athletes' generosity or community service. In these cases, the media and PR staff try to inform the public of positive events and how they positively reflect back on the team. In the case of an incident that might be perceived negatively by the public, such as the trade of a player or the firing of a coach, the PR specialist informs the public of the facts and the position of the team and attempts to minimize any negative effect on the organization.

Whom You Will Work With

Media and PR specialists have the unique advantage of working with many people within the organization. They work with the athletes, gathering information and insight about them so they can help them relate to the public. They work with coaches, learning about the team and team strategy, including potential draft picks and trades, so they can relay information to the media and public appropriately. They work with marketing and upper management to coordinate communications about the team, and sometimes to coordinate press releases and media information with events or marketing campaigns. If, for example, a former athlete was going to rejoin the team in a coaching capacity, the PR specialist might coordinate the release of that information with a significant marketing promotion such as the former athlete's jersey retirement.

The media and PR staff also work with newspapers, magazines, radio, television, and other media outlets to disseminate information. Sometimes this means writing a press release; other times it might mean arranging an interview, press conference, or news coverage of a player or the team. In today's Internet-based media environment, a media and PR specialist will also often work with a web design and technical support team to design and maintain the team's website. In fact, many sport organizations have a web specialist as one part of their overall media and PR team.

What Personal Skills and Abilities You Will Need to Succeed

The primary skills that media and PR career specialists need are strong writing and speaking skills. A media and PR specialist must be able to communicate clearly using both written and spoken words. A person in this position must also be creative, able to come up with new angles and new ideas for campaigns and projects. Flexibility is an asset, because many last-minute issues arise when covering a sport team, so it is imperative for PR specialists to think on their feet and adjust to unanticipated opportunities and challenges.

What Education and Certifications You Will Need

Media and PR specialists generally have strong training in journalism or communications. A background in sport is helpful; you must be able to speak and write intelligently and credibly about sport experiences. Courses such as media and public relations in sport, sport marketing, and communications can help build this educational base. From a technical aspect, web design training and computer skills have become increasingly important. These need not be formally trained, but those coming into a PR career with web design experience can certainly gain an advantage in the job market.

Future Outlook

Job growth in the media and public relations area is expected to resemble that of sport marketing (about 13 percent growth by 2018). According to Kathy Babiak, a researcher in sport management at the University of Michigan, one thing seems sure: these positions will remain essential to organizations because they help the organization enhance their reputation through community outreach. Especially among nonprofit organizations, media and PR specialists will be essential partners in development efforts and in encouraging people to use the organization's services. For example, following the lead of professional sport organizations, many parks and recreation departments are employing PR specialists to generate interest in their facilities and programs to maximize their use so that they remain central and sustainable within the community.

PROFESSIONAL SCOUT

The job of professional scout is one of the oldest and most interesting positions in sport. In professional leagues, there are usually three types of scouts: an amateur scout, a professional scout, and an advance scout. Amateur and professional scouts observe and evaluate prospective talent for their teams, whereas advance scouts observe and evaluate upcoming opponents.

Where You Will Work

Like most jobs in sport, the job of a professional scout is seasonal. In the off-season, scouts spend a little time off, then are back to work scouring developmental and rookie leagues for potential talent. During this period, they generally live in their hometown. In the preseason, scouts spend time with their own team, talking to newly acquired ball players and preparing for the upcoming season. During this period, they live wherever the team does their preseason training. During the season, most scouts spend nearly every night on the road—either watching potential talent or, if they are advance scouts, watching opponents' games. Although they can eat well, travel in style, and stay in nice hotels, veteran scouts typically spend over 200 nights per year on the road. Those new to the game should be prepared to drive many miles, eat lots of fast food, and sleep on many hard beds while out on the road doing their job.

What You Will Do

Amateur scouts spend their time assessing amateur talent, which could include high school athletes (in baseball, basketball, and hockey, especially) and college athletes. Generally these are nondrafted athletes that the teams might like to acquire. In addition to evaluating talent, amateur scouts spend time in the players' homes discussing salary requirements and determining general fit for the team. They make recommendations to the scouting coordinator and to the general manager about amateur players they think the team should draft and in what rounds.

Professional scouts spend their time assessing professional talent that teams might like to acquire. This pool of talent includes both minor or developmental leaguers as well as professional players who are likely to become free agents or be traded. For example, in baseball, a professional scout will monitor minor leagues, rookie leagues, Mexican and Dominican leagues, and the major leagues, with most of his focus on the minor leagues. This individual watches a tremendous amount of baseball and makes recommendations to the general manager about whom the team should try to acquire via trades and free agency.

An advance scout travels in advance of the team to scout upcoming opponents. Although the role of the advance scout has changed over time, particularly with the advances in video technology, most teams still like to have someone (or more than one) watch their opponents live. Scouts watch formations and patterns of formations. They watch athletes' skills and tendencies. They watch for strategy, preferences, and potential weaknesses. All of this information is transferred to the position coach, the head coach, or the general manager so that game strategies can be developed or enhanced.

Whom You Will Work With

Professional scouts work mainly with upper team management and with the athletes themselves. At the amateur level, scouts work with athletes, their parents, coaches, and agents to examine the athlete's interest and fit with the team and the amount of money needed to sign the player. At the professional level, scouts are not allowed to speak with athletes or their agents unless the athlete is a free agent in a signing period. At all other times, the scouts spend their time evaluating players and communicating with general managers so that when a trade or acquisition opportunity arises, the general manager knows who the team wants to acquire. Much of the time, however, scouts work alone, traveling from city to city watching athletes and games.

Gene Watson

Scouting coordinator for the Kansas City Royals

Gene Watson has been working in baseball for over 20 years. He says, "In baseball, the three most important keys for success in scouting are a passion for the game, the ability to recover from mistakes, and a relentless pursuit of the profession. Scouting is very subjective, and you have to be ok to make mistakes and move on to the next decision. You have to be willing to do what others will not and do not let your ego stop you from doing whatever the team asks you to do."

What Personal Skills and Abilities You Will Need to Succeed

Professional scouts say the primary traits needed for success are love for the sport, perseverance, and flexibility. Scouts spend so much time immersed in their sport, enduring long days on the road, that they must really love doing what they do. They must also have a player's knowledge of the game so they are credible with athletes and have a good sense of the skills, both physical and mental, necessary for success. The profession of scout is highly desirable and competitive, so you must persevere to obtain an initial position. Good scouts are flexible and teachable.

What Education and Certifications You Will Need

As is true of many careers in sport management, there are no certifications for the job of a professional scout, although some leagues or teams will require scouts to pass examinations about league rules before hiring them. Good communication skills and an ability to evaluate talent are the primary skills needed in this career. Further, a sport management degree can help scouts understand the basics of rules and contracts (e.g., courses in sport law) and can help one gain an understanding of the overall and financial operations of a professional club (e.g., strategic management, sport finance). This may assist a scout in seeing the bigger picture of the club and help him or her advance to higher management positions.

Future Outlook

According to the USDL, we may expect the demands for scouts (and coaches) to increase by about 25 percent over the next 10 years. This depends, of course, on the health and growth of college and professional leagues. However, scouting positions remain highly competitive, which might limit salary growth. For example, in 2009, the median income for a professional scout was $28,340 (U.S.), while the lower 10 percent earned only $15,530. According to professional scouts, time in the profession is brief, so entry positions are available with some frequency, but upward mobility can be limited.

SPORT EVENT MANAGER

Sport event managers plan and conduct sport events with and for sport teams or organizations. These events range from pregame tailgate parties for university alumni, to draft celebrations for star college players, to activities leading up to participating in a Super Bowl, and even to the ultimate event, the Olympic Games.

Where You Will Work

Much like sport marketers, sport event managers work for full-service event management firms, professional teams, or colleges or universities. In fact, in many ways the working conditions for a sport marketer and an event manager are quite similar—seasonal, very long hours during the playing season, more office and planning hours during the off-season, and typically a very enjoyable atmosphere.

Event managers who work for professional teams usually have more of an on-and-off season; those who work for a college or full-service events are likely to have a steady year-round schedule. Consider, for example, the event staff at the University of Texas. During the fall, they plan and carry out events for football, soccer, cross-country, and volleyball. Often, they prepare and host postseason tournaments for soccer and volleyball. Then, starting in November, they begin hosting events for basketball, swimming and diving, and indoor track and field. They assist coaches in hosting major tournaments and NCAA postseason tournaments. In the spring, they work with tennis, golf, baseball, and track and field. Thus their schedule involves a year-round flow of games, regular-season tournaments, and postseason events.

Individuals who work for a full-service event management firm will probably find themselves traveling to events, and perhaps even living in event cities in advance of the event. For example, Super Bowl planners move to the host city in August prior to the event (in January or February) so they can plan locally and acquire and train volunteers for both the game and its ancillary events. Other event organizers might not live in the host city but will make several extended visits prior to the event. Conversely, if working for a team or a university, sport event managers might complete the majority of their work in their home city.

Salaries at the university or professional level range from $40,000 to $80,000 (U.S.), depending on the size of the university and the number of events conducted. Salaries for a full-service event firm range from $60,000 to $170,000, again depending on the scope of the job and the associated events.

What You Will Do

At universities, sport event managers plan and conduct multiple events throughout the year. Event planners at the professional level may spend their entire year planning one event, as is the case for the Super Bowl. So jobs can vary widely even within an event specialty. Event planners must operate within an overall concept of the event or an event design; this usually begins with establishing the time, date, and scope of the event. This might be followed by developing a planning checklist or procedures manual for the event that involves all the people, places, and things needed to make the event successful (see figure 5.1 for a sample checklist). A checklist might cover flowers and signage, volunteers, a band, food, drink, security, and garbage removal. The planner then spends significant time putting all necessary pieces into place. As the event draws closer, he or she confirms plans and training staff for each of their roles. This staff might include volunteers who require training; proper training can be a critical component to event success. Consider a recent mixed martial arts event. The volunteer staff arrived the day before the event to receive training in facility design and emergency procedures so they could answer patrons' questions (e.g., Where are the restrooms? Where are my seats? Where is the concessions stand?) and manage basic emergencies that might occur during the course of the event.

Event Set-Up List

1. Fill a cooler to be set up in the goal patrol area with ice and water.
   - Coolers are located in the storage room, and the water, ice, and cups are in the training room.
2. Fill a cooler with ice and cold drinks for the event staff; set it up near the sign-in area.
   - Coolers and drinks are located in the storage room. Ice is in the training room.
3. Set up tables throughout the stadium.
   - Marketing table (1) is located just inside gate 4.
   - Player pass table (1) is located just inside gate 1.
   - Longhorn goal patrol table (1) is set up inside the birthday/goal patrol area.
   - Tables for birthday parties are set up inside the birthday/goal patrol area when needed (quantity varies).
   - Tables are located at the end of each team bench for the trainers (total of two).
   - A small table is set up on the track at midfield.
4. Set up chairs throughout the stadium.
   - Chairs (6) are located in the track area for ushers (4) and EMT (2).
   - Chairs (2) are set up at the player pass table.
   - Chairs (3) are set up at the marketing table.
   - Chairs (2) are set up at the midfield table.
   - Chairs (varies) are set up in the birthday party area.
5. Bring headset, substitute sign, and air horns to the midfield table.
   - The headset plugs into an outlet located directly behind the table at the opposite edge of the track near the railing.
6. Attach Soccer Autograph Alley, Texas Soccer All-Americans, NCAA, Texas Soccer, Big 12 signs to metal barricades (located at the north end of the track) using cable ties.

During the Event

1. Ticket takers: everyone who enters the stadium must have a ticket except for students. Students do not need tickets and can be let in at any gate. Keep track of all student patrons by clicking them in on your clicker. There must be a ticket taker at the gates *at all times*.
2. Scoreboard operator: start the clock at the appropriate time; check in with the events director.
3. Upper/lower concourse ushers: constantly walk up and down the corridor. Your job is to make sure children are not in the throwing area playing a soccer game of their own. Make sure no children have decided that a fun place to cool off is in the ice machine. Also pay attention to the ushers on the track; they will alert you to situations in the stands that need attention.
4. Ushers on the track: you do not have to face the crowd at all times, but you are responsible for keeping an eye on the crowd and making sure that everyone in the stands is abiding by the rules during the event.
5. Track entrance/field house usher and SID ladder usher: make sure the only people on the track are the team, media, officials. *No* patrons! There must always be someone at this position; if you need to be relieved, radio someone to take your place.

Halftime/Duration of the Game

1. There are three gates with at least three ticket takers at each gate during halftime.
   - First ticket taker: Collect the stubs from all three ticket takers at your gate and the student clickers. Count all of your stubs and your student numbers and radio the player pass table with your two numbers.
   - Second and third ticket takers: Once you have given all of your ticket stubs and clicker to the first ticket taker, go to the field and relieve one of the six ushers on the track.
   - Once everyone has been relieved on the track and at the field house entrance, all staff should return to original positions for the duration of the game.
2. Player pass workers: After all the numbers have been collected and reported to the supervisor, the player pass table and chairs should be broken down and stored in the ticket office at gate 1. Once your duties are over, you are to relieve anyone that needs a break before the game ends.
3. Ten minutes before the game is over, ticket takers at the gates should collect their stools and put them in the ticket office. Gate 4, you are also responsible for putting away the marketing table and chairs, along with your stools. Also, if there was any use of pop-up tents during the event, you are responsible for storing those before the game ends.
4. Ushers on the track are to stay in position until the end of the game.

Post Event

IF WE WIN:

1. One ticket taker must remain at each gate to hand out promotional coupons.
2. The remaining staff should come down to the track and start to line the field to prepare for autographs:
   - Ticket takers
   - Lower concourse usher
   - Upper concourse usher
   - Player pass
   - SID ladder
3. Ushers on the track should remain at their stations and make sure no one tries to get on the track. Usher all patrons to the track entrance to line up for autographs. Once all fans are out of the stands, come toward the autograph session.
4. All event staff are to keep people off the field and from walking or wandering down the track toward the field house. Patrons should be asked to leave through gates 1 or 4. If they must leave through gate 3, they have to walk under the stands to get to the gate; they cannot walk down the track.
5. I will need four event staff members to collect the chairs on the track, tables, and my clear plastic box and put them away *during* the autograph session.
6. When autographs are finished, all of the table and chairs should be put away and everyone should sign out together.

IF WE DON'T WIN:

Everything stays the same, but we do not hand out promotional coupons. We just say good bye to the patrons as they leave.

Figure 5.1 Sample planning checklist for a NCAA soccer match.

Devon Hendricks

Events director at the University of Texas at Austin

People who thrive in this career enjoy the details and the variety of responsibilities, from training volunteers, to taking tickets, to texting VIPs with directions to the event. The ability to express yourself clearly and efficiently is a must. Hendricks says the following about being successful in the field: "Event managers must have impeccable planning and organizational skills, which includes the ability to think through every need and contingency for the event, and the ability to track the progress of each event facet from design through implementation."

© Human Kinetics

Following each event, most event managers conduct a follow-up analysis and evaluation. This includes an examination of the design, process, procedures, personnel, and finances of the event. What did they do well? What could be improved? Should we seek other vendors? Did we reach our financial goals? How well were problems handled? Did people enjoy the event? These questions help event managers plan better for future events.

Whom You Will Work With

Sport event managers work with all kinds of people. In fact, event managers claim one of the most enjoyable aspects of their career is the variety of people they work with, and the experience they gain from them. Consider an event planner for the Final Four men's basketball tournament. He or she might work with *everyone*—team managers and coaches, alumni, flower vendors, hotel personnel, limousine drivers, food and beverage providers, even college presidents. Event managers coordinate with upper management and often with the marketing department to ensure that events are aligned with the overall mission of the organization and with themes and concepts developed by the marketing department. Event managers might also work with sponsors to ensure the event lives up to the sponsor's expectations.

What Personal Skills and Abilities You Will Need to Succeed

Event managers need organizational and communication skills, the ability to problem-solve in action, and the knack of maintaining a sense of calm in the midst of chaos. Events rarely go exactly as planned, so event managers must be able to think on their feet and make quick decisions, often in the midst of the event. What happens if the team's flight is cancelled and they cannot arrive for the event? What if attendance was underestimated and the food and beverage is insufficient? What if the fourth pillar will not come out of the stage to complete the Olympic torch? An event manager must be able to make quick decisions and adjustments so the event can continue smoothly and successfully.

What Education and Certifications You Will Need

No certifications are required, but many organizations recommend some type of emergency management training as well as training in CPR and first aid. In terms of

Star Student: Jenna

Photo courtesy of Jenna Moor.

I feel the most important aspect of succeeding in the sport industry as a student and aspiring sport manager is creating relationships and continuing to keep these connections in order to build a networking profile with various individuals. It is also critical to begin to research internship opportunities early and to get involved in sport somewhere, whether it be volunteering for events or working part time for an organization. This kind of experience will show your dedication to sport and help you build a résumé that will be enticing to employers. Finally, being proactive and continuing to search for new opportunities as a student is my biggest advice for any individual seeking a future in sport. The best opportunities I have experienced are those in which I took the initiative to contact organization leaders to express my interest in learning and eagerness to get involved.

Jenna, graduate student in sport management

formal education, a background in sport management is excellent training for this field. Courses such as sport and special event management, facility management for sport, sport finance, and human resource management provide a sport event manager with the education and training to manage and coordinate the people, money, and facilities needed for a successful events operation.

Future Outlook

The future for sport event managers looks promising, especially for those willing to expand their expertise beyond just sporting events to other events as well. For example, in a full-service event firm, you might need to plan and conduct sporting events as well as concerts, circuses, banquets, and conventions. According to the U.S. Department of Labor and the Convention Industry Council, jobs in this specialization are expected to increase about 20 percent over the next 10 years. Opportunities will be greatest for individuals with a bachelor's degree and some event experience. While in their undergraduate programs, students are encouraged to find volunteer opportunities, part-time work, or internships in event planning to gain experience.

SPORT MEDIA SPECIALIST

Careers in sport media include jobs such as journalists, photographers, television camera operators, and sound crew members. The job of a sport journalist entails learning and writing about or reporting sport news. Similarly, sport photographers capture pictures that complement written stories or tell stories in themselves. Sport journalists might work via the Internet, print media, television, or radio, with most new jobs focusing on new forms of media, including Internet news, blogging, and other more instant news outlets. Similarly, photographers use both print and Internet media to communicate their work. Camera operators and sound crews work behind the scenes to produce programming and sometimes to support in-stadium operations. Sport media is an exciting career for those interested in the personal side of sports and in exploring new technology for communications.

Where You Will Work

In the past, sport journalists have typically worked in a newsroom or private office where they have access to computers, televisions, wire reports, telephones, and fax machines. As technology advances, sport journalists are increasingly able to work from home or on the road. Often rookie journalists work from the newsroom or on the road, whereas veterans gain more flexibility in their work environments. Depending on the position, most sport journalists spend considerable time outside the office covering stories and watching sporting events.

Sport photographers and camera crews, however, spend most of their time at the games covering or producing the event. They might be hired locally to cover different types of events or might travel in crews (e.g., ESPN) around the country covering only one or two events per week. Sound crews, in particular, might be hired by a single team and work in only that team's venue to provide video and sound augmentation to games or events.

Although some photographers and camera crews work year-round, covering whatever sport is in season, the work is often seasonal because most journalists specialize in a particular area of sport, such as college basketball or WNBA. Like other jobs in sport, work during the season tends to be more demanding than in the off-season, although off-seasons still require effort and planning. For example, sportswriters who cover college football and basketball begin their seasons in late July or early August and work steadily through the end of March. In April through June there is still work to do and stories to cover, but hours are usually more regular and there is not as much travel. Writers on general assignment, however, are not seasonal but can remain busy year-round. Others in sport careers might have more of a routine, but this is not typical in the journalism profession. Because news cannot be predicted, journalists must learn to be flexible and always in response mode.

According to the Newspaper Guild, a print journalist makes in the range of $50,000 to $80,000 (U.S.) a year depending on the size of the city and the newspaper. This salary range is similar for full-time online or television sport journalists. Experienced and freelance sport journalists can make significantly more, especially if they also write sport books. Photographers and camera operators can also be employed independently or by a network, media outlet (e.g., *Sports Illustrated*), or team. As such, their pay varies widely. An experienced camera operator can make $500 (U.S.) per day, yet often carries his or her own expenses. If employed by a network, they can make $60,000 to $80,000 annually and will probably cover multiple sports and events.

What You Will Do

Sport journalists and photographers write, capture, or report on games and events or interesting issues related to sport that occur off the field. Thus one part of a journalist's job is to go on the road and cover events. For example, a journalist or photographer might be assigned to cover the Super Bowl and its ancillary events (practices, fan reactions, team headquarters, etc.), but might also write a story about a player's family, disharmony among members of a team, or the increasing role of religion in sport. Sport journalists also work in television, where they write copy for television sport shows or for sportscasters. Often print journalists are assigned stories by their editors, but some veteran journalists are given more flexibility. Photographers might work with a print journalist to cover a story; they might take their photos independently and have them chosen (by an editor) to complement a written story; or the photos might be chosen independently to stand alone as their own story.

Sportwriters spend a great deal of time at events, usually writing their stories as they develop on the court or field. When they are not at events, they spend time on the telephone, e-mailing, and interviewing people to get background, facts, and opinions for their stories. They might call athletic directors, coaches, agents, or general managers or talk to sport information or media directors. Sometimes they have to hop on a plane and travel to the source.

Camera operators and sound crews spend their time at the events capturing the actual event. They might also spend considerable time travelling, maintaining their equipment, and working on production schemes. Sound crews, especially those housed in a stadium, spend considerable time outside of the games producing videos and other content to use at the games. They also operate the sound at the games, ensuring all technical specifications are met and quality is high.

Whom You Will Work With

Sport media specialists work with whomever is essential to their stories. This can lead to interesting and exciting opportunities—ones the media specialist might never have predicted. Relatively inexperienced sport writers work primarily with sport information and media directors to obtain information and access to people inside the organization. Experienced sport journalists, especially those who had been in the same niche, would more likely contact the coaches, agents, or top executives directly. Print journalists and photographers work with other writers and the section editor to coordinate stories and assignments, to develop writing or photographic skills, and to evaluate performances. Television and radio journalists work with production staffs, camera and sound crews, and on-air talent. Online sportswriters tend to make their contacts with sources and then write from their home offices.

What Personal Skills and Abilities You Will Need to Succeed

Camera operators and sound crew members require mostly technical skills and the ability to work with others. They need to be able to operate highly technical equipment and to coordinate with other camera operators and production crew. Sport journalists need to write well. If you do not enjoy writing, avoid this career. Sport journalists tend to be outgoing and likable. Sport photographers also require great photographic skills—both creative and technical. Adept photography requires much practice.

Sport journalists need to know more than just sports and how to play them. They need to know the issues, the rules, and the background of the sport so they can identify when issues are important or misaligned. Sportswriters who plan to write on issues within sports need to understand the larger role of sport in society as well as the history surrounding a sport. Course work in sport sociology and sport history is helpful. Journalists who write about college and professional sports might also benefit from basic coursework in law and criminal processes. Understanding commerce or educational law, for example, helps writers doing stories on labor or union issues, steroid regulations, or tax regulations of the NCAA. Sport has an integrated position in society, and it is important to be able to identify and integrate such coverage.

Steve Wieberg

Veteran sportswriter for *USA Today*

According to Wieberg, "A sport journalist needs to be competitive, inquisitive, and a little bit cynical (i.e., questioning what is going on with a story). A journalist always needs to be trying to get at the 'real' story, things that don't look right, smell right, seem right."

What Education and Certifications You Will Need

Whereas in the past, individuals with an English or similar degree who were good writers could just as easily enter the journalism profession, in today's news era, specific training in a journalism school is becoming increasingly necessary. Sport journalism, like any area of journalism, is best learned in a journalism program. Journalism schools provide training not only in print or visual media but also in emerging technology. Today's journalist spends only a small portion of time on print media. Journalists are now expected to produce stories for blogs, Twitter, Facebook, online chats, and so on. In fact, many journalists now carry personal video devices when covering a story so they can include video of their interviews or events with the online content.

Perhaps the perfect educational preparation for a sport journalist is a double major in journalism and sport management or sport studies or a major in journalism with a minor in sport management or sport studies. Courses such as sport history, critical issues and events in current sport, sport and society, governance of sport, or race and gender in sport are valuable for providing a background in sport to supplement the on-field coverage of the sport itself.

Future Outlook

The outlook for in-print journalists and traditional beat writers is currently stagnant and possibly in decline, but the overall outlook for the profession is bright, especially for those who can adapt to emerging developments in news media and those with specializations in a particular media niche. As specialization becomes increasingly important in the journalism market, students with knowledge and experience in sports have an advantage in the sport journalism market. New writers might find they need to produce freelance stories and articles to provide employment.

SPORT FACILITY OPERATIONS MANAGER

One of the most engaging and hands-on type of work in sport is that of a facility operations manager. This individual is in charge of handling all the behind-the-scenes details necessary for a sport facility to present its events and for players and fans to have enjoyable experiences.

Where You Will Work

A facility operations manager works at the venue he or she manages. Typically, there is not much travel involved because the bulk of attention is paid to the actual facility. Hours per week depend heavily on the time of season and the number of events and teams housed in the facility. For example, facility managers of a minor league baseball stadium can expect very long hours during baseball season; on game day, the facility operations manager is often the first one to arrive and the last one to leave the stadium. However, during the off-season, when the venue is fairly quiet, the hours are much more limited. In a venue like the Pepsi Center in Denver or the American Airlines Center in Dallas, however, the hours are more demanding, because the venue is full nearly every night with events ranging from professional basketball and hockey to circuses and rock concerts.

According to PayScale, a facility manager could expect to make between $37,000 and $83,000 (U.S.), with an average of $55,000. Managers of larger venues with more event dates of course earn larger salaries than those at smaller venues with fewer events.

What You Will Do

Each event requires staffing, security, venue configuration, food and beverage sales, lighting, maintenance, and trash removal. The facility operations manager is responsible for all these aspects. He or she makes sure that the event is staffed with ushers, ticket takers, and enough personnel to run the event. The manager makes sure enough people are trained properly to answer fan's questions and tend to the athletes and coaches as necessary. The facility manager is also responsible for security, a growing concern in large venues. In many cases, facilities hire a full-time security manager in addition to the operations manager.

One of the most interesting aspects of the facility manager's job, especially in a multiuse facility is venue configuration. In a single-use facility such as a baseball stadium, facility operations managers must configure areas of the stadium for meetings, concerts, and other events so the facility can be used for purposes other than baseball games. How do you manage a shift from a hockey game one night, to basketball the next, to a rock concert with specialized lighting and stage design two days later? How do you transform a football stadium into a rodeo arena? These are challenges faced by facility operations managers. The facility operations manager also coordinates all food and beverage sales for the events. This might include in-house operations for stadium suites and club sections, as well as general vending and concessions for all patrons, which is usually outsourced to a concessionaire such as Marriot or Aramark. Finally, the facility operations manager is in charge of the facility itself, ensuring that lighting is optimal, the facility is clean and well maintained, damages are repaired, bathrooms are clean and in working order, the playing surface is healthy and well maintained, and so on. All of these responsibilities require year-round attention.

Star Student: John

Photo courtesy of John McConnell.

At the beginning of my sophomore year in college I knew I wanted to do something in the sport industry, I just didn't know what yet. While most of my peers weren't even beginning to think about doing an internship, after talking to my advisor, I decided it would be worthwhile to do one even though I was only a sophomore and most people waited until they were seniors. There was an opening in operations at a new facility, and I landed it. Working in this internship for a full three years (instead of the usual single semester that most students do) was instrumental in my getting the full-time position I landed right out of college. My experience as an intern enabled me to build key relationships within the athletic department and be more qualified and more experienced than any of the 102 other people who applied for the position. For any aspiring sport managers, I cannot emphasize enough how important it is to land a good internship, both for figuring out what you want to do and for giving you the experience necessary to achieve your goals.

> *John, assistant director of operations in a college athletic department (BA in kinesiology, sport management)*

Whom You Will Work With

Because facility operations managers have a hand in many different tasks, they work with a wide variety of people, including maintenance personnel, who repair and maintain the facility; event staff, either directly or through a staffing organization to make sure they have sufficient and well-trained staff; and with a concessionaire to determine the types and amount of food and beverage to be sold. They also work with event managers to determine facility needs; security personnel (including local police) to establish security needs and procedures in and around the facility; and possibly turf, floor, dirt, or other playing surface vendors and experts to determine the types of surfaces best suited to their facility and the proper care and maintenance thereof.

What Personal Skills and Abilities You Will Need to Succeed

Facility operations managers must be flexible, willing to learn, well organized, able to solve problems quickly, and able to communicate clearly with a variety of people. They must also have some skill at facility maintenance because they might need to make minor adjustments and last-minute repairs. They need good spatial awareness to understand how people and things fit together in a space, and how the space will look when it is occupied. This allows them to make adjustments as necessary, such as moving events to a different section or larger room, or moving equipment to make more space, or changing traffic flow patterns to avoid long lines or congestion in important areas. They must also be in good physical condition because the job often requires climbing stairs or traversing large stadiums or arenas several times a day.

What Education and Certifications You Will Need

The expected educational background for a sport facility manager is similar to that of a sport event manager. In some cases a background in turf or surface management can be an asset. A facility operations manager needs a good background in communications, human resource management, financial management, and risk management. A major in sport management with a minor in agriculture (turf management) or risk management would be particularly suited for this career.

Future Outlook

According to the USDL, job growth in sport facility operations is expected to be about as fast as the national average for most other jobs. In addition to job growth, the International Facility Managers Association forecasts that facility managers jobs will grow increasingly complex as issues such as environmental sustainability, security, and globalization become more tightly linked to the facility manager's position. As with many jobs in sport, more specialization and more experience (even as a student) will provide an advantage in securing employment and advancement in this career.

Chapter 6

Careers in Sports Medicine

Jolene M. Henning, EdD, ATC, LAT

Sports medicine is an umbrella term that covers a variety of health-related careers including athletic training, exercise physiology, sports nutrition, and aquatic therapy. Sports medicine professionals use a team approach to providing health care for physically active patients and often collaborate to deliver quality services that allow individuals to return to all levels of physical activity, from activities of daily living to competitive sport. Those interested in combining the excitement of physical activity and sport with the scientific fields of health and medicine naturally gravitate toward the many possible careers in sports medicine.

CERTIFIED ATHLETIC TRAINERS

Athletic training encompasses the prevention, diagnosis, and intervention of emergency, acute, and chronic medical conditions involving impairment, functional limitations, and disabilities. This broad expertise allows the athletic trainer (AT) to be uniquely qualified to provide health care from the moment an injury occurs all the way through to the point of return to competition. The title "athletic trainer" can be misleading, implying that these individuals work only with athletes. That is not the case. Athletic trainers work with physically active patients of all ages and activity levels. Also, do not confuse athletic trainers with personal trainers, who are fitness professionals, not health care providers (for information on personal trainers, see chapter 3).

What Education and Certifications You Will Need

All certified athletic trainers, regardless of employment setting, must earn a degree from an accredited athletic training education program. The Commission on Accreditation of Athletic Training Education (CAATE) is the only agency that accredits programs of this kind. In a CAATE-accredited program students are instructed in eight content areas (listed in figure 6.1) and receive extensive hands-on clinical instruction working with athletes and other physically active patients. Individuals who graduate from a CAATE-accredited program are eligible to sit for the Board of Certification (BOC) examination for entry-level athletic trainers. The BOC is the only agency that certifies athletic trainers and provides the credential of certified athletic trainer (ATC). After earning the ATC credential, most athletic trainers who want to work in a collegiate setting seek further education in either an advanced master's degree program in athletic training or a related field, such as sport psychology or biomechanics.

Future Outlook

The U.S. Department of Labor's Bureau of Labor Statistics estimates that employment of athletic trainers is projected to grow 37 percent from 2008 to 2018, much faster than the average for all occupations. This expectation is because of the role of ATs in preventing injuries and reducing health care costs (www.bls.gov). It is predicted that employment opportunities in colleges will remain steady while high schools, hospitals, and sports medicine clinics will see a rise in jobs for athletic trainers. Athletic trainers are also expanding job opportunities in several emerging practice settings, such as the armed forces, public service agencies (e.g., FBI, police), and the performing arts.

Athletic Training Educational Competencies for CAATE Accredited Programs

Evidence-based practice

Prevention and health promotion

Clinical examination and diagnosis

Acute care of injury and illness

Therapeutic interventions

Psychosocial strategies and referral

Health care administration

Professional development and responsibility

Reprinted from NATA 2011.

Figure 6.1 Athletic trainers receive extensive classroom and clinical education related to eight major content areas while enrolled in CAATE-accredited athletic training education programs.

Star Student: Drew

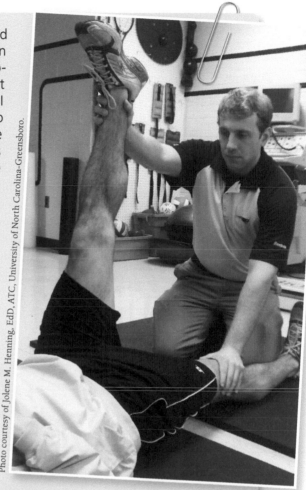

The excitement associated with professional sports often attracts students to the profession of athletic training, and that is what happened for me, too. I was fortunate enough to get to experience firsthand what it is like to work with professional athletes when I was invited to complete two summer internships with the New England Patriots. One thing I learned is that to become an effective athletic trainer you must dedicate yourself to the profession. This means taking your education and clinical development seriously. Use every opportunity given you to improve as a clinician. Be able to combine both the knowledge learned in class and in clinical rotations to further your overall professional development. The NFL has great internship opportunities that introduce future professionals to the life of athletic trainers in the NFL. My experience with the New England Patriots taught me the value of working as a team when providing health care to elite athletes. I also learned the importance of having a strong work ethic, maintaining a positive attitude, and obtaining the ability to adapt to new situations. Professional characteristics important to being a successful athletic trainer include effective communication skills, time management, and dependability.

Photo courtesy of Jolene M. Henning, EdD, ATC, University of North Carolina-Greensboro.

Drew, master of science in athletic training (MSAT) student

College and University Athletic Trainers

Where You Will Work

One of the most popular employers of athletic trainers is the college and university setting; in fact, according to the National Athletic Trainers' Association (NATA), 24 percent of ATs work in the collegiate setting. ATs in this setting work directly with intercollegiate athletes on a daily basis providing on-site medical care during team practices and games. An exciting aspect of the collegiate environment is the opportunity to travel with athletic teams to games and tournaments (e.g., NCAA basketball tournament, football bowl games, etc). Athletic trainers in this setting typically work more than 40 hours per week, including evenings and weekends. According to a 2008 survey conducted by the NATA, the average salary for all collegiate athletic trainers is approximately $39,000 (U.S.).

What You Will Do

A typical day for an AT in the collegiate setting includes an exciting array of activities that might differ on a daily basis—no day is ever the same! Collegiate ATs typically fill their mornings providing rehabilitation services for injured athletes (e.g., postsurgical ACL rehabilitation). In the afternoons they turn their focus to injury prevention by preparing athletes for team practices, guiding them through stretching and strengthening protocols. The majority of an AT's afternoon and evening is spent providing medical coverage at practices or games. During this time the AT evaluates and diagnoses injuries and provides treatment and emergency management of injuries. ATs in this setting also make critical return-to-participation decisions following injuries.

Erica Thornton

Head AT at the University of North Carolina at Greensboro

Thornton knows firsthand what it takes to succeed in this setting: "Any athletic trainer employed in a college setting will be faced with juggling multiple tasks simultaneously, and must be able to prioritize appropriately as well as employ time-management skills in order to be efficient and productive. It's important to be empathetic and comfortable dealing with a diverse population, all while working toward the same goal of returning to competitive athletics. The rewards of working in a team setting are numerous; however, it is beneficial to be flexible and maintain a sense of humor to better tolerate the early mornings and late nights you experience while in season."

Photo courtesy of Jolene M. Henning, EdD, ATC, University of North Carolina-Greensboro.

Whom You Will Work With

ATs in the collegiate setting work under the guidance of orthopedic surgeons and other physicians. They collaborate with strength and conditioning specialists, sports nutritionists, and sports psychology consultants. Coaches rely heavily on ATs to make return-to-participation decisions for their athletes.

What Personal Skills and Abilities You Will Need to Succeed

The collegiate athletic training setting is a very fast-paced environment and requires an appropriate sense of urgency in returning athletes to a competitive level of participation. For example, if an athlete is injured during a game situation, the AT must be able to quickly determine if the injury is significant enough to prohibit return to the game or if further activity will not exacerbate the condition.

Athletic Trainer for a Sports Medicine Clinic

Where You Will Work

The most prevalent employers of ATs are sports medicine and outpatient rehabilitation clinics. According to the NATA, about 28 percent of ATs work in a clinic setting. In this setting athletic trainers treat and rehabilitate patients of all ages and physical activity levels. For example, patients could range from a 25-year-old recreational softball player with shoulder pain to a 55-year-old factory worker with an overuse condition in his elbow.

What You Will Do

The primary duties of an AT in a clinic are to provide treatment using therapeutic modalities (e.g., ice, heat, electrical stimulation, and ultrasound) and conduct rehabilitation sessions for patients suffering from orthopedic injuries. Unlike in the collegiate setting, ATs in a clinic do not typically provide medical coverage for athletic teams on a regular basis.

Whom You Will Work With

Athletic trainers in a clinic work closely with physical therapists, occupational therapists, and orthopedic surgeons. Most outpatient rehabilitation clinics use a collaborative approach to health care that relies on the different expertise of these individuals to deliver the most comprehensive approach to providing patient care.

What Personal Skills and Abilities You Will Need to Succeed

Athletic trainers working in sports medicine or outpatient rehabilitation clinics interact with patients from all walks of life and varying levels of physical activity. Working with such a variety of patients requires ATs in a clinic to be knowledgeable of medical conditions (e.g., diabetes, heart disease) that might be confounding factors in delivering rehabilitation services to the lay population.

Kris Burns

Athletic trainer at Greensboro Orthopedics

Burns has worked as an athletic trainer in the clinic setting for nine years and can attest to the qualities needed to be successful in this environment: "In order to be a successful clinical athletic trainer, communication is critical. You have to find a common denominator with your patients and be able to communicate in a way that allows you to gain their trust. You need to have empathy for your patients, understand their goals, keep things fresh and never lose your own passion for learning in order to keep your skills current."

Athletic Trainer in a High School

Where You Will Work

High school athletic departments have hired the services of athletic trainers for decades. Approximately 26 percent of certified ATs work in the high school setting, making it the second most popular employment setting for ATs. The work day for a high school athletic trainer includes providing medical coverage for afterschool interscholastic athletic events that often extend into the evening or weekend hours. Some ATs also work at sports medicine clinics during the morning hours and at a high school in the afternoon. With these responsibilities combined, athletic trainers in public high schools earn an average of $43,000 (U.S.) per year.

What You Will Do

There is a great deal of public interest in reducing the rate of injuries in adolescent athletes. The AT is a critical link in coordinating injury prevention efforts in the high school setting. One of the most common duties of an AT in a high school is to provide medical coverage for collision sports such as football and lacrosse because of their high risk of injuries. Athletic trainers are the first person on the scene when an injury occurs and so must be highly efficient in emergency management and acute care of injuries. In addition to working with football and lacrosse teams, ATs also juggle a high volume of patients made up of student-athletes from other teams, such as soccer, basketball, and baseball teams. Because of the broad spectrum of athletic practices and games occurring on any given day after school, the AT must be flexible and able to supervise multiple events at once.

Whom You Will Work With

The health care team in a high school is usually relatively small and might consist of only one athletic trainer, supervised indirectly by a physician. As a result, ATs in high schools might find it advantageous to train coaches in first-aid and CPR in the event that the AT cannot be physically present at all practices and games that

Doug Bauman

Athletic trainer at De La Salle High School in Concord, CA

In his position, Bauman appreciates that "above being knowledgeable, personable, and possessing excellent educational skills, the most important quality of a high school athletic trainer is the ability and desire to act as a mentor to student-athletes."

Photo courtesy of Doug Bauman.

occur simultaneously. This ensures that coaches are at least minimally trained in recognizing emergency situations.

What Personal Skills and Abilities You Will Need to Succeed

Athletic trainers in the high school setting have the unique opportunity to work closely with impressionable student-athletes and must understand the physical and emotional development of this age group. High school ATs typically seek out workshops or conferences that focus on injuries prevalent in athletes under the age of 18 in order to better understand the nuances of the maturing human body and how injury can affect musculoskeletal development.

Athletic Trainer as a Physician Extender

Where You Will Work

Athletic trainers working in orthopedic physician offices are often called physician extenders because they work in conjunction with orthopedic surgeons, extending their services and creating opportunities to treat more patients in a shorter period of time. This is a relatively new role for athletic trainers, and the NATA does not have specific membership data to represent the number of ATs working in this capacity; however, use of the AT in this context is an emerging trend in orthopedic offices, and the number of jobs will likely increase as physicians continue to boost their productivity as a result of the presence of ATs working as physician extenders. Physician extenders typically work 40 hours per week and earn approximately $46,000 (U.S.) per year.

What You Will Do

Athletic trainers hired as physician extenders are usually the first point of contact with a patient in an orthopedic office. ATs triage patients by obtaining a medical history and performing an initial musculoskeletal assessment before the patient

Ben Williams

Physician extender at Greensboro Orthopedic Center in Greensboro, NC

Williams works side by side with orthopedic surgeons and primary care physicians and knows firsthand what it takes to thrive in that environment. "To be successful as a physician extender, an athletic trainer must have a strong foundation in both history-taking and physical examination, the ability to multitask and adapt to changing situations, and excellent communication skills when dealing with both patients and physicians."

Photo courtesy of Ben Williams.

sees the physician. The AT presents the patient's case to the physician for final diagnosis and to determine a plan of care. In addition to traditional professional preparation as a certified athletic trainer, ATs in the role of physician extender also have specialized training in casting, splinting, and brace fitting. ATs in this role also provide gait training and patient education for home therapeutic exercise programs.

Whom You Will Work With

Along with working side by side with orthopedic surgeons, physician extenders collaborate with family practice physicians, physician assistants, radiology technicians, and orthopedic technicians.

What Personal Skills and Abilities You Will Need to Succeed

Functioning as a physician extender is an exciting new role for athletic trainers. In addition to the traditional clinical skills required of athletic trainers, those who function as physician extenders receive on-the-job training in applying and removing fracture casts, advanced bracing techniques, and assisting physicians with applying sutures.

CLINICAL EXERCISE PHYSIOLOGIST

Registered clinical exercise physiologists (RCEP) are health care providers who work primarily with patients diagnosed with chronic diseases who have been referred by a physician for an exercise prescription as a form of complementary treatment. RCEPs are trained to work with patients with cardiovascular and pulmonary diseases; metabolic disorders, such as diabetes; cancer; and immunological disorders. RCEPs also develop exercise prescriptions for healthy individuals in order to prevent disease (e.g., cardiovascular disease). The U.S. Department of Labor does not track salary data for RCEPs, but according to Payscale.com, earnings are on average about $40,000 (U.S.) per year.

Where You Will Work

Clinical exercise physiologists work primarily in hospital and clinic settings under the supervision of a licensed physician. Facilities that offer cardiac or pulmonary rehabilitation programs and exercise oncology services employ the services of a RCEP. Community-based agencies such as the YMCA often offer exercise programs supervised by a RCEP, and some might be involved in conducting research in exercise testing laboratories to determine the most effective exercise prescriptions for certain diseases.

What You Will Do

To prescribe effective exercise programs for patients, RCEPs conduct and interpret data from exercise testing to determine the body's normal and abnormal response to exercise. RCEPs evaluate patients' ability to perform aerobic and anaerobic exercise and assess their muscular strength and endurance, flexibility, and ability to perform common functional tasks. RCEPs interpret this information and work in conjunction with physicians to develop the most effective protocol for each patient and to provide exercise counseling services.

Whom You Will Work With

In addition to being supervised by a licensed physician, RCEPs collaborate with nurses, nurse practitioners, and physician assistants. They oversee clinical exercise specialists (CES), who often manage the day-to-day exercise progression of a patient. All of these health care providers collaborate to provide a comprehensive exercise plan for patients suffering from cardiovascular disease, diabetes, or other long-term health conditions.

What Personal Skills and Abilities You Will Need to Succeed

Working with patients who have chronic health problems often requires a multidisciplinary approach to health care. RCEPs are one piece of the puzzle in helping patients return to a higher quality of life. Because of the collaborative nature

Cody Sipes, PhD

Co-owner of Miracles Fitness in West Lafayette, IN

Sipes has been a registered CEP for 10 years. He says that "being an RCEP requires the ability to interact professionally with nurses, physicians, and therapists as well as personally with patients and clients from all walks of life. An RCEP must be observant, able to quickly analyze a situation and respond appropriately."

of treating patients with chronic diseases, it is imperative that RCEPs be able to accurately interpret exercise stress tests, EKGs, and other measures of health and fitness and communicate those results effectively to other health care providers. RCEPs must also be able to educate their patients on healthy lifestyle choices.

What Education and Certifications You Will Need

Clinical exercise physiologists must earn a master's degree in exercise physiology or kinesiology. The Clinical Exercise Physiology Association—an affiliate of the American College of Sports Medicine (ACSM)—requires a minimum of 600 hours of supervised clinical experiences (table 6.1) or a previous certification as a CEP in order to take the ACSM examination to earn the credential as an RCEP. Certification in CPR as a professional rescuer or basic life support provider is also required.

Table 6.1 Recommended Patient Contact Hours for RCEP Exam Eligibility

Cardiovascular patients	200 hours
Pulmonary patients	100 hours
Metabolic patients	120 hours
Orthopedic/musculoskeletal patients	100 hours
Neuromuscular patients	40 hours
Immunological/hematological patients	40 hours

Future Outlook

The U.S. Department of Labor does not track the job outlook for RCEPs, but the high rate of obesity in the United States combined with the aging of the population will continue to create a need for RCEPs to work with diabetic and cardiopulmonary rehabilitation patients, among others, in years to come.

CERTIFIED CLINICAL EXERCISE SPECIALIST

Certified clinical exercise specialists (CES) are health care professionals who work primarily with cardiac and pulmonary rehabilitation patients. CES professionals often work hand in hand with registered clinical exercise physiologists (RCEP) but do not treat the breadth of patients seen by a RCEP. A CES performs exercise testing and data interpretation for patients at risk for or recovering from cardiovascular diseases.

Where You Will Work

Clinical exercise specialists work in hospitals and clinics that offer cardiac and pulmonary rehabilitation services. Hospitals with in-patient cardiac rehabilitation services quickly integrate CES professionals into the care plan of patients who have undergone heart catheterization, angioplasty, or have received cardiac stents. Most CES professionals work in outpatient cardiac and pulmonary rehabilitation programs offered through hospitals or community-based agencies such as the YMCA. According to Payscale.com, the average entry-level CES earns $31,000 (U.S.) a year.

What You Will Do

The goal of a CES is to create an individualized exercise plan that addresses the physical needs of each patient. To create such plans, the CES must be highly skilled in performing tests used to implement and modify patients' exercise prescriptions. For example, CES professionals monitor blood pressure, blood glucose, and heart rate before and after physical activity. They assess cardiovascular endurance, strength, flexibility, and body composition. An important aspect of daily tasks for a CES is to educate patients on the role of exercise in rehabilitation, how to properly execute exercise techniques, and how to modify their lifestyle to incorporate physical activity.

Whom You Will Work With

Clinical exercise specialists work under the guidance of a physician's prescription to provide cardiac and/or pulmonary rehabilitation for patients. Thus they must be able to communicate effectively with physicians about patients' progress or regression and determine how to modify the exercise plan appropriately. Other typical colleagues of a CES are nurses, registered dieticians, registered clinical exercise physiologists, respiratory therapists, and psychologists.

What Personal Skills and Abilities You Will Need to Succeed

Clinical exercise specialists are a critical link in the prevention and rehabilitation of patients at risk for or diagnosed with cardiovascular and pulmonary diseases. In addition to technical training in exercise testing and exercise prescription, a CES must be sensitive to the physical and emotional needs of patients who have suffered a life-altering event (e.g., heart attack). CES professionals should also be well versed in assisting patients with establishing realistic exercise goals and lifestyle changes while educating them on the relation between these factors and disease prevention. The CES strikes a delicate balance between facilitating behavior change in patients and not overwhelming them with too much technical information.

What Education and Certifications You Will Need

The ACSM offers the only certification for clinical exercise specialists. If you are interested in pursuing the CES credential, you should follow specific steps. First, you must earn a bachelor's degree in kinesiology or other exercise-based degree. The degree must include courses in anatomy, physiology, exercise physiology, biomechanics, exercise prescription, and fitness testing. You must also gain practical experience in a clinical exercise program (figure 6.2) and have current certification as a basic life support provider or CPR for the professional rescuer. On completion of these prerequisites, you will be eligible to take the ACSM exam to become a certified CES.

- Minimum of 400 hours from a COAES* accredited university curriculum program
  OR
- Minimum of 500 hours from a non-COAES accredited university curriculum program
- It is recommended that practical experience in a clinical exercise program include the following:
  - Cardiac/pulmonary rehabilitation
  - Exercise testing
  - Exercise prescription
  - Electrocardiography
  - Patient education and counseling
  - Disease management of cardiac, pulmonary, and metabolic diseases
  - Emergency management

*COAES—Committee on Accreditation for the Exercise Sciences

Figure 6.2   Practical experience required for CES certification.

Future Outlook

The USDL does not track employment data on clinical exercise specialists. Unfortunately, the Center for Disease Control reports that obesity rates in the United States continue to rise, resulting in an increased risk for cardiopulmonary and other diseases. This creates a continued need for certified clinical exercise specialists trained in cardiac and pulmonary rehabilitation.

SPORT DIETICIAN

There is an increasing focus on the role of proper nutrition and the use of dietary supplements in optimizing athletic performance. This has created a need for nutrition professionals who can specialize in individual nutrition counseling for competitive athletes. Sports nutrition is a relatively new specialization in the broader field of nutrition and dietetics that is growing in popularity. To avoid confusion it is important to note the differences between a dietician and a nutritionist. A dietician is a nationally credentialed registered dietician (RD) with an extensive academic and clinical background in the science and practical application of food and nutrition principles. The title "nutritionist" is vague and often used by individuals with a background in nutrition who are not registered dieticians. Employers are most likely to hire an RD rather than a self-proclaimed nutritionist who may or may not have the appropriate background to provide nutrition counseling. So if you want to specialize in sports nutrition, plan to become a registered dietician and then take the appropriate steps to become a certified specialist in sports dietetics (CSSD).

Where You Will Work

Employment settings for CSSD professionals are expanding. Many collegiate athletic departments and professional sports teams hire part-time or full-time sports dieticians to counsel athletes on proper nutrition for training and competition and, as necessary, to assist with managing athletes with eating disorders. Sport dieticians also provide nutrition education in academic settings (e.g., teaching at a university) and in fitness and wellness facilities. One of the most popular employment opportunities for CSSD professionals is in private consulting. Typically these individuals also have academic preparation in kinesiology and can offer combined services in nutritional counseling and weight management.

What You Will Do

The clientele for CSSD professionals range from fitness enthusiasts to elite athletes, so the type of services provided varies from client to client. For example, marathon runners and triathletes have very different nutritional needs from those of a college football player. Sport dieticians work one on one with athletes to analyze their current nutrition status, develop nutrition goals, and implement dietary changes. Sport dieticians educate their clients on proper dietary intake and supplement use to maximize their athletic performance.

Whom You Will Work With

CSSD professionals in a collegiate or professional sports setting typically work in collaboration with athletic trainers, physicians, and coaches to develop nutritional strategies for individual athletes and sports teams. Those engaged in private practice obtain clients through advertisement and referrals from physicians or other health care professionals in the community.

What Personal Skills and Abilities You Will Need to Succeed

Because most CSSD professionals are consultants, it is necessary to have an entrepreneurial spirit and high level of self-motivation in order to seek out clients who could benefit from a sports dietician. Because CSSDs work with such a wide range of physically active clients they must be sensitive to individual needs and goals. For example, a freshman collegiate football lineman might need assistance developing a nutrition plan that allows for healthy weight gain to meet the higher physical demands of the sport at the collegiate level compared to the high school level. On the other hand, someone training to compete in an ultra-endurance race (e.g., the Ironman) might need assistance in developing a nutrition plan that meets the body's demands for engaging in very long bouts of physical activity.

What Education and Certifications You Will Need

The process of becoming a registered dietician and CSSD involves four steps. First, you must graduate from an undergraduate program accredited by the Commission on Accreditation for Dietetics Education (CADE) within the American Dietetic Association. The second step is to complete a 900-hour clinical internship supervised by registered dieticians. This can be completed either through an accredited internship in dietetics after you receive a four-year degree or through what is called a coordinated program. A coordinated program combines the undergraduate degree with the internship experience. The most popular method for completing an internship is through the accredited internship option. The final step in becoming an RD is to pass the national board exam for dieticians. It is only after you pass the board exam that you can legally use the RD credential. Registered dieticians with a particular interest in sports nutrition can earn the certified specialist in sports dietetics (CSSD) certification. The requirements for becoming a CSSD (listed in figure 6.3) are established by the Commission on Dietetic Registration.

- Be a current registered dietician (RD) for a minimum of two years
- Documentation of 1,500 hours of specialty practice experience in sports nutrition as an RD within the past five years

Figure 6.3   Eligibility requirements for certified specialist in sports dietetics (CSSD).

Kimberly C. Schorn

Board-certified specialist in sports dietetics

Schorn runs a private consulting business that combines dietetics, exercise physiology, and lifestyle/behavior change strategies. As a CSSD, Kimberly provides dietetic services for recreational to elite athletes. "As a sports dietitian you must have a passion for fitness and nutrition, and a strong desire to work with athletes. It's definitely a fast-paced, high-energy environment that's always on the go and changing every day in teaching different groups how to fuel effectively. When it comes down to it, trust me, there's nothing like seeing an athlete make the big play and win the game . . . and know that you were a part of that. Talk about an amazing feeling!"

Future Outlook

The Commission on Dietetic Registration reports that there are currently fewer than 350 registered dieticians with the additional CSSD credential. The U.S. Department of Labor does not monitor employment data for sports dieticians separate from registered dieticians. In general, average employment growth is projected for RDs, and the Bureau of Labor Statistics indicates that dietitians with specialized training, an advanced degree, or certifications (such as the CSSD credential) beyond the minimum requirement will experience the best job opportunities.

SPORTS MEDICINE CLINIC AND CENTER DIRECTOR

As is true for every business, health care facilities need good managers to keep operations running smoothly and effectively. Sports medicine clinics are no different. Clinic directors work long hours and must be adept at navigating the ever-changing health care delivery system that is regulated at the state and federal levels. Whereas some health care administrators are considered *generalists* and oversee large facilities or integrated systems, it is more common in the realm of sports medicine to utilize specialized *clinical* directors or managers. These individuals have training or experience in a specific clinical area (e.g., physical therapy) and manage a facility that provides that particular service. In addition to their specialized training as therapists, clinical directors often have additional training in business management. The U.S. Department of Labor reports that the average annual income for health care administrators in outpatient rehabilitation centers is about $74,000 (U.S.).

Where You Will Work

Clinical directors typically work in outpatient rehabilitation centers or sports medicine clinics. Clinics of this nature are either owned independently or have a physician partnership with an orthopedic group. Health care administrators who are more generalists might work in large hospital facilities or even oversee an entire hospital system.

What You Will Do

Clinic directors are involved in all facets of managing a health care facility. They establish and implement policies and procedures, hire and evaluate personnel, and develop budget reports and contracts with insurance companies. Most clinic directors also continue to treat patients in the facility, which allows for rapport among colleagues.

Whom You Will Work With

Sports medicine clinic directors work with a variety of personnel, including office staff (e.g., administrative assistants, insurance coordinators), patient care providers (e.g., physical therapists, occupational therapists, athletic trainers), and physicians. Directors build rapport with product vendors, insurance companies, and community supporters. Working with such a vast array of people requires the director to have exceptional interpersonal skills.

What Personal Skills and Abilities You Will Need to Succeed

Because they are ultimately responsible for the efficiency of patient care provided by their staff, clinic directors must possess strong leadership and management skills. They must also be able to multitask and tolerate high levels of stress related

John W. O'Halloran

Director of physical therapy and sports medicine at Southeastern Orthopedics in Greensboro, NC

As a physical therapist and athletic trainer with over 24 years of experience in the field of sports medicine, O'Halloran can attest to the skills needed to be successful as a clinic director: "The personal qualities necessary for a clinical director of sports medicine are daily preparation of patient flow for yourself and your staff. You also need to have an uncanny ability to anticipate schedule quirks and business interruptions. For example, after a long holiday weekend many patients forget their appointment time and come in earlier or later than scheduled. You have to prepare for this and train your staff accordingly. Professional qualities are that as a clinic director it is imperative that your clinical skill set parallels your business growth model. For example, you need to stay current clinically and maintain or acquire postgraduate certifications and skills as you develop your staff's and facilities services."

to supervising other clinicians and office personnel, coordinating and processing insurance claims, and ensuring patients have positive clinical outcomes.

What Education and Certifications You Will Need

The educational preparation of sports medicine clinic directors varies. At a minimum, clinic directors have a bachelor's degree in a health-related field. Most directors are also credentialed health care providers (e.g., physical therapists) and have completed extensive graduate work in their specialization. It is helpful to seek continuing education in health care administration or management principles to better understand the business side of health care delivery.

Future Outlook

According to the U.S. Bureau of Labor Statistics, director and manager positions in all health care settings will continue to rise in order to improve quality and efficiency health care delivery while controlling costs. With the passage of health care reform in the United States, it is estimated that the need for clinic directors who can navigate changing insurance regulations will grow in the future.

AQUATIC THERAPY SPECIALIST

Aquatic therapy is an umbrella term used to describe water-based therapeutic exercises designed to improve functional activities. The Aquatic Therapy and Rehab Institute specifically defines aquatic therapy as "the use of water and specifically designed activity by qualified personnel to aid in the restoration, extension, maintenance and quality of function for persons with acute, transient, or chronic disabilities, syndromes or diseases." Patients with a variety of injuries and conditions benefit from the freedom of movement made possible by the buoyancy of water; this makes aquatic therapy a beneficial adjunctive therapy that does not create additional stress and strain on joints. Aquatic therapy should not be confused with aquatic fitness (aquatic exercise focused on overall general health and wellness) or adapted aquatics (aquatic activity for persons with disabilities). Health care providers specializing in this area are typically credentialed in other subdisciplines, such as physical therapy, occupational therapy, or athletic training, and have sought additional training in the application of aquatic therapy.

Where You Will Work

Aquatic therapy specialists work in traditional outpatient rehabilitation centers, hospitals, and sports medicine clinics that have access to a full-size or therapeutic-size pool. The aquatic therapy specialist is considered an add-on certification for other health care providers such as athletic trainers and physical therapists. Thus it is difficult to speculate exactly how many individuals have obtained this certification. As well, although salary data is not available for these professionals, it can be assumed that salary ranges are similar to other health care providers employed in sports medicine rehabilitation clinics.

What You Will Do

Aquatic therapy specialists work with a variety of patients using aquatic-based exercises as an adjunct to traditional therapeutic interventions. For example, it is common for physical therapists to integrate aquatic therapy into the walking progression for patients recovering from total knee replacement surgery because the buoyancy of the water allows for an earlier progression than does walking on land. Aquatic therapy specialists incorporate principles of water and physics into the development of therapeutic exercise protocols for maximum patient outcomes.

Whom You Will Work With

As mentioned previously, aquatic therapy specialists are typically credentialed health care providers in other areas and thereby work in collaboration with other physical therapists, occupational therapists, athletic trainers, and exercise physiologists. They work with patients who have orthopedic conditions ranging from total hip replacement to rotator cuff repair as well as general health conditions such as cardiovascular disease.

What Personal Skills and Abilities You Will Need to Succeed

Aquatic therapy specialists must be good communicators and enjoy working one on one with patients. They must have a high level of creativity in order to determine how land-based rehabilitation exercises can be modified for performance in water.

Julie Hutchins

Athletic trainer at Southeastern Orthopedic Specialists in Greensboro, NC

© Human Kinetics

Hutchins incorporates aquatic therapy into her treatment regimen with many of her patients. "I love aquatic therapy. If feasible, I would put every one of my patients in the water. I have seen firsthand the benefits that result from the safe environment of the water, in reducing swelling, increasing motion and strength, and improving confidence. Most of all, aquatic therapy allows individuals to succeed and return to their lives. The physical and emotional benefit patients gain from the water is a great complement to any therapy program."

What Education and Certifications You Will Need

There are various certifications in the aquatics industry but only one that targets aquatic therapy. The Aquatic Therapy and Rehab Institute (ATRI) certification verifies that therapists are competent and knowledgeable in the industry standards for aquatic therapy and rehabilitation (see figure 6.2). Eligibility to take the ATRI certification exam includes completing 15 hours of education in aquatic therapy, rehabilitation, or aquatic therapeutic exercise education. Therapists can complete this education through hands-on or online courses.

Standards for the Aquatic Therapy and Rehabilitation Industry (Summarized)

- Have knowledge in key areas:
  - Movement mechanics and science
  - Aquatic principles
  - Aquatic therapy and rehabilitation basic principles and methods
  - Applicable regulations and legal considerations
- Exhibit professional responsibility
- Demonstrate health and safety consciousness

Figure 6.4 The Aquatic Therapy and Rehab Institute (ATRI) certification requires that therapists are knowledgeable in key concepts related to the theoretical background and application of aquatics with injured patients.

Future Outlook

Because aquatic therapy specialists are typically also certified or licensed as other health care providers, the U.S. Bureau of Labor Statistics does not specifically track employment of professionals in this area. In addition, insurance companies are less likely to reimburse clinics for aquatic therapy services, so the market demand for specialists has declined in recent years. However, with the passage of federal health care reform it is possible that this trend will reverse and the demand for aquatic therapy specialists will rise.

Chapter 7

Kinesiology as Pre-Professional Training for Allied Health Sciences

V. Dianne Ulibarri

Obtaining an undergraduate degree in kinesiology as pre-professional training for a career in the health sciences has become one of the most popular goals for students majoring in kinesiology. The term *pre-professional* means that a program is a stepping stone to advanced study in a related area. Why major in kinesiology if you want to go into a health-related career? Primarily because of the core of science courses required in the kinesiology major. Kinesiology is the only field that focuses on the movements and functions of the human body from the collective viewpoint of dynamic anatomy; biomechanics; exercise physiology; motor control, development, and learning; psychology; and sociology. Often physics and chemistry are prerequisites to some of these courses. In many cases, the information covered in these courses is similar to the information covered in the first years of most of the health care professions. From this broad base of knowledge, undergraduate kinesiology graduates can more easily learn and apply the concepts taught in these graduate health-related programs. Given the rigor and thoroughness of kinesiology programs, it is not surprising that kinesiology graduates have a high success rate in completing graduate study in the health care professions and finding careers in these areas.

Examples of the health care fields I am referring to include but are not limited to physical, occupational, and exercise therapies; medical and osteopathic physicians and surgery; chiropractic; dentistry; nursing; physician assistants; nurse practitioners; and other medical providers. There are many similarities across these professions, including the work environments, duties, and additional education and certification necessary for licensure. However, the same common individual characteristics exist across all health care fields. Ideally, all these professionals have personality traits of compassion, patience, concern for others, dependability, responsibility, high ethical values, and integrity. They exhibit self-control, cooperation, independence, and adaptability. One intangible component of these professions is "heart"—a deep passion for serving others and helping them improve their health and well-being.

All of the health care professions require practitioners to have excellent communication skills. These skills are active listening, clear writing and speaking skills, reading comprehension, speech clarity and recognition, and strong oral expression. These individuals also must be competent in monitoring patients, managing time, planning and prioritizing, thinking critically, making decisions and judgments, reasoning both inductively and deductively, and problem solving. Work activities include assisting and caring for others, obtaining information, documenting and recording information, leading others, and establishing and maintaining interpersonal relationships with peers, clients, and patients. Future employment opportunities in all of these health-related areas are above average according to the Bureau of Labor Statistics.

PHYSICAL THERAPIST

Physical therapists (PTs) work with patients to restore, maintain, and improve function, alleviate pain, and prevent dysfunction by accurately diagnosing and treating musculoskeletal or neurological disorders affecting movement. PTs might work with diseased patients, patients recovering from surgery, and patients recovering from accidents or strokes. They assess movement capabilities, design rehabilitation regimens, monitor patient progress, and communicate with physicians regarding patients' progress.

Where You Will Work

Physical therapists work in a variety of health care environments, including hospitals, orthopedic settings, private offices, schools, and clinics, and some offer consulting services. They work with clients ranging in age from infants to the elderly and from physically skilled elite athletes to couch potatoes. Most work a 40-hour week, including early mornings, evenings, and weekends to accommodate their clients' schedules. About one third of all PTs work part time. In general, PTs who work in hospitals, clinics, and rehabilitation settings have a more regular work schedule than those who own their own business, where they might need to work evenings and weekends to accommodate patients' schedules. Physical therapy is in demand in virtually all nations, so some licensed therapists obtain work visas from various countries and travel the world, finding employment in hospitals and rehabilitation centers abroad.

The most recent data from the Bureau of Labor Statistics indicate that the median annual wage for physical therapists is $72,790 (U.S.). The range for wages for the middle 50 percent is between $60,300 and $85,540. The lowest 10 percent earned less than $50,350, and the highest 10 percent earned more than $104,350.

What You Will Do

Physical therapists have many responsibilities, roles, and functions. The three primary responsibilities are evaluating and diagnosing, developing and delivering treatment plans, and preventing loss of mobility. The physical therapist is responsible for conducting an initial examination to identify and diagnose problems. Flexibility and strength; motor function, development, and control; functional capacity; and circulatory and respiratory efficiency are within their test protocols. Following this diagnosis, the PT develops an individualized plan to address the problem(s), set goals, and follow the progress of the patient. Continued reevaluation is critical because the treatment plan must usually be adjusted to achieve the goals. Record is made of the treatment modalities used, the patient's response to the treatment, and the progress of the client. The PT instructs the patient and family on the treatment plan to follow. Reassessment is vital and includes the medical practitioners and others to plan, administer, and evaluate the treatment plan. PTs must keep up on the latest software and equipment development and applications.

Whom You Will Work With

Physical therapists are constantly communicating and working with other medical professionals, including physicians, podiatrists, prosthetists, dentists, nurses, social workers, psychologists, and occupational and speech therapists. They also communicate with family and friends within the confines of regulations regarding patient privacy.

What Personal Skills and Abilities You Will Need to Succeed

In addition to the general abilities required of all health care professionals, physical therapists need physical stamina and strength because it is necessary for them to stand and walk for long periods, move equipment, and lift and assist patients as they walk, move from a lower to a higher position, and turn. The patient needs assistance in these activities because of muscle weakness and balance problems.

Physical therapists should also have strong interpersonal and communication skills in order to educate patients about their condition and treatments, and to communicate with patients' families. Physical therapists must be compassionate and possess a strong desire to help patients.

Jolynn Nelson, MS

Physical therapist

Nelson, who works in a rehabilitative setting, tells would-be
physical therapists: "You need to
be a sleuth to get the whole picture—questioning, listening to,
and observing the dance of questions, and then knowing where
the answers fit in. You also need
to understand and genuinely care
about the patient."

Photo courtesy of Physical Therapy at Mindful Movement and Physical Therapy

What Education and Certifications You Will Need

The Commission on Accreditation of Physical Therapy Education (CAPTE) is the American Physical Therapy Association's (APTA) accrediting body. In 2009, there were 212 physical therapy programs in the United States. Two hundred of these schools award doctoral degrees, or the Doctorate in Physical Therapy (DPT). Most students complete DPT programs in three years. Although master's degree programs exist (which take two to two and a half years to complete), the PT taking this route is limited to working under a physician's direction rather than working independently.

Physical therapy education programs include many of the basic science foundation courses found in undergraduate kinesiology programs: anatomy, physics, biomechanics, chemistry, exercise physiology, motor control/development/learning, psychology, and statistics. Thus a kinesiology degree might meet most of the prerequisites for admission to a graduate program in physical therapy. However, additional coursework in your undergraduate program might be required; most students embarking on a physical therapy career ensure that they take these courses as electives during their undergraduate years. Physical therapy coursework ranges from foundational courses in biology and cellular histology, to neuroscience, pharmacology, pathology, and radiology/imaging. Courses in behavioral science dealing with evidence-based practice and clinical reasoning, and clinical based coursework include medical screening, examination tests and measures, diagnostics, interventions, outcomes assessment, and the business of managing a practice. Supervised clinical experience is also part of the program. Most physical therapy programs require volunteer experience in physical therapy prior to acceptance into the program.

States regulate the practice of physical therapy, and eligibility requirements differ by state. Typical requirements for physical therapists include graduation from an accredited physical therapy education program, passing the National Physical Therapy Examination, and fulfilling state requirements. Many states require continuing education as a condition of maintaining licensure. Physical therapists participate in continuing education courses and workshops, thereby continuing their professional development.

Star Student: Laura

Photo courtesy of Laura Gibson.

In earning a kinesiology degree I have developed a strong background in human anatomy, exercise physiology, biomechanics, and human development, which has provided a deeper understanding of difficult course content. This deeper understanding has made it easier to meet graduate program challenges. For example, a biomechanics kinesiology course allowed advanced comprehension of complex arthrokinematics for a graduate course on human joints. I was already familiar with human joint concepts such as the common planes of body movements, the rules of convexity and concavity, and the expected movements of certain joints. This basic understanding allowed me to concentrate on the more advanced aspects of the course.

In addition to biomechanics-related material, my kinesiology preparation has also provided a solid foundation for human anatomy lecture and cadaver lab graduate courses. An extensive portion of the first year of physical therapy school is spent learning human anatomy. In class it was helpful to understand muscles and ligaments in regards to functional activities. Applying anatomy knowledge to functional activities is important because sometimes patients might only be able to report that a particular activity is painful. The physical therapist must then consider which anatomical structures could be involved. Having a kinesiology degree makes this thought process more efficient and less dependent on memorization.

My kinesiology degree has not only prepared me for academic success but has also allowed me to test out of some graduate courses. This saved me thousands of dollars in tuition and allowed me to focus on and better understand other coursework and to participate in research. My degree in kinesiology has been an important step toward my goal of working as a physical therapist.

Laura, DPT student

Some physical therapists become board certified in a clinical specialty. The American Board of Physical Therapy Residency and Fellowship Education (ABPTRFE) is responsible for credentialing post-professional clinical residency or fellowship programs. This credentialing is voluntary and designed to recognize programs that significantly advance a PT's knowledge and skills in patient–client management within an area of practice.

Future Outlook

A 30-percent job growth for physical therapists is expected by 2018, for a number of reasons. The expected increase in the geriatric population along with the debilitating and chronic problems that accompany advanced age is a primary reason. Changes in restrictions for third-party payer reimbursements have increased and will continue to increase patient demand. Developments in medicine and technology leading to a greater number of survivals across a wide range of injuries and illnesses will also create the need for rehabilitative care. Job opportunities will be good in all settings, particularly in environments where the elderly are most often treated. Job openings should be plentiful in rural areas.

OCCUPATIONAL THERAPIST

Occupational therapists use treatments to assist their patients in leading independent lives. Some patients need treatment to develop, regain, or maintain work-related and daily living skills. They help clients compensate for permanent loss of function, as well as improve basic motor and neurological functions and reasoning abilities. The goal of the occupational therapist is to help patients reach or return to their full potential for leading full, productive lives. The roles of the occupational therapist and physical therapist are often confused, and in many respects they do overlap. According to the American Occupational Therapy Association, OTs are trained to view patients holistically within their daily activities, across each patient's lifespan. OTs develop a variety of programs for their clients. For example, physical well-being for children is addressed through play activities, and seniors are taught modified activities to prevent falls and to assist in daily living movements. One way to think about the two professions is that occupational therapists treat clients with a wide range of cognitive, developmental, emotional, and physical abilities, whereas physical therapists' treatments are focused more on specific physical disabilities.

Where You Will Work

Work environments for occupational therapists include many of the same locations as for physical therapists. Occupational therapists work in hospitals, clinics, outpatient care services, home health agencies, nursing care facilities, community rehabilitation and mental health centers, schools, government agencies, and private practices. They also work in job training, adult-care programs, driver re-education programs, prisons, and in community and production-based organizations concerned with ergonomics and design, leisure activities, and disability accommodations. An increasing number of occupational therapists are being hired by school districts, where they provide direct service to students as well as consult with parents, administrators, and other school staff on matters related to the design of learning environments.

As is the case for physical therapists, the OT's work is demanding. They are on their feet much of the time, and they must lift and help transport clients and equipment. An OT working for a single employer works a traditional 40-hour week. Travel time between facilities needs to be considered for OTs who work for different employers or at different locations for the same employer. Those OTs working in schools might find they need to attend meetings with administrators, parents, and students throughout the day.

In their most recent report, the Bureau of Labor Statistics reported that the median annual wage for OTs was $66,780 (U.S.). The wages for the middle 50 percent ranged between $55,090 and $81,290. The lowest 10 percent earned less than $42,820, whereas the highest 10 percent earned more than $98,310.

What You Will Do

Occupational therapists, collaborating with clients, are responsible for initial evaluations and development of the intervention plan. They then implement the intervention plan and, as the client progresses, determine whether the plan needs to be continued, modified, or discontinued. OTs are responsible for outcome evaluations and direct the entire evaluation process, as well as all aspects of the initial client contact. This initial OT evaluation includes need for the service, defining the problem within the OT domain that needs to be addressed, determining the client's goals and priorities, establishing intervention priorities, determining further assessment needs, and determining assessment tasks that can be delegated to the OT assistant. Finally, the OT is responsible for selecting, measuring, and interpreting outcomes related to the client's ability to engage in occupations. The OT also takes on supervisory roles to OT assistants and aides. The OT is responsible for interpreting information provided by the OT assistant and integrating pertinent information into the ongoing evaluation and decision-making process.

Their work requires that OTs often employ computer programs to retrain brain function, improve abstract reasoning and perceptual skills, and enhance sequencing and coordination—skills important for continued independent living. Some OTs focus on individuals with behavioral problems and disorders, such as substance abuse or eating disorders; others focus on stress-related disorders; still others specialize in helping clients engage in active lives and cope with everyday stresses. Some teach time-management skills, budgeting, homemaking, and the use of public transportation; others evaluate daily living needs, in home and work or school settings, in order to make recommendations for changes in those environments that will assist in continued productivity. Occupational therapists identify home hazards, such as throw rugs that contribute to falls, and make recommendations for installing grab bars in the bathtub and handrails for stairs, especially in older homes. Teaching clients or patients to use crutches, walkers, prosthetics and fitting splints or braces are all responsibilities of the OT. Educating family members and caregivers as necessary is another common and important duty.

Whom You Will Work With

OTs work with other individuals in the health care professions, including but not limited to physical therapists; primary care physicians; physical, mental health, and speech therapists; nurses; physician assistants; and nurses' aides. They might also work with administrators and parents or employers in the school or work setting. They might collaborate with design engineers to build and use computer-aided adaptive equipment for communication improvement and to better control different situations in their client's environment. Some building contractors employ OTs to assist in the design of rehabilitation facilities.

Occupational therapists work with clients who have temporary, congenital, or permanent mental, physical, emotional, or developmentally challenging conditions. OTs may choose to treat only a select age or disability group. An example might be a group of patients needing to return to work following a work-related accident, or a client who has had a traumatic, serious, life-changing health condition, such as stroke, brain injury, heart attack, or amputation. Their patient base might be those who have learning and developmental disabilities and mental health illnesses, or conditions such as Alzheimer's disease or posttraumatic stress syndrome. Unlike physical therapists, occupational therapists often treat patients with brain function abnormalities, helping them improve their short-term memory, visual and perceptual skills, decision making, pattern recognition, and problem-solving skills.

What Personal Skills and Abilities You Will Need to Succeed

The personal skills needed to be an OT are the same as for the PT and other health professionals. Listening, as well as speaking, reading, and writing communication skills are critical, as are assessment and evaluation skills. Compassion, time management, patience, use of a variety of computer software programs, counseling skills, and business and management skills are essential. The OT must also have good social skills to open up communication channels with clients, families, and employers.

What Education and Certifications You Will Need

All states regulate the practice of occupational therapy. Like physical therapists, occupational therapists must be licensed, and that requires a master's degree or higher degree in OT from an academic program accredited by the Accreditation Council for Occupational Therapy Education (ACOTE). Licensure also requires passing of a national certification exam. On passing the exam, the individual becomes an occupational therapist registered (OTR). Note that passing the national exam does not necessarily meet all the requirements for licensure in all states. Each state has its own requirements for licensure; these requirements can be obtained from each state's licensing board.

Once therapists have the OTR designation, they are encouraged to continue professional development by participating in workshops and classes. Some states require continuing education as a condition for maintaining a license in that state. Further certification may be required, especially for OTs involved in intervention programs.

In 2009, the Bureau of Labor Statistics reported that there were 150 accredited master's degree programs, or combined bachelor's and master's degree programs. There are only four accredited OT doctoral degree programs in the United States.

Star Student: Brittany

Photo courtesy of Brittany Bremenour.

Earning an undergraduate degree in kinesiology gave me the tools I needed to transition into graduate study in occupational therapy. The science and research-based curriculum of kinesiology closely follows the basic components of graduate study in occupational therapy. From this curriculum, I developed the knowledge and professionalism essential to further my education and enter the health care field. My kinesiology degree has provided opportunities to gain familiarity with a variety of areas, including anatomy, physiology, and psychology. Studying in a human cadaver laboratory and having experiences in an exercise physiology setting are unique features of kinesiology that prepared me for graduate courses such as neurology and future fieldwork placements in the community. The high expectations and requirements involved in obtaining a degree in kinesiology promote a strong work ethic and the development of organizational skills that I use both in and out of the classroom. The focus that kinesiology has on human movement gives me a greater understanding of how movement affects functioning in daily life, which will be crucial to the treatment that I will provide for future clients. Ultimately, the depth and breadth of a kinesiology degree sets it apart from other undergraduate programs and establishes a solid foundation for many prospective fields.

Brittany, Occupational Therapy Graduate Student

Most programs are traditional full-time programs. Recently there has been an increase in the number of OT schools offering part-time programs, including evenings and weekends. Coursework includes biological, physical, and behavioral sciences, as well as courses in application of theory and skills unique to occupational therapy. All accredited programs require at least 24 weeks of supervised fieldwork. Program administrators prefer applicants who have already completed paid or voluntary experiences in occupational therapy. In most cases, undergraduate majors in kinesiology have the broad knowledge base leading to successful completion of an advanced degree in occupational therapy.

Future Outlook

According to the Bureau of Labor Statistics, the job outlook for OTs is expected to grow by 20 to 26 percent by 2018, especially for those therapists interested in working with the elderly and in the area of business consulting. It is estimated that growth in the geriatric population will increase demand for therapeutic services. Working with the elderly will have a significant effect on job opportunities for occupational therapists. Job opportunities for OTs will also benefit from an anticipated increase in the number of individuals with disabilities or limited function. Medical advances have extended the lives of patients, many of whom are in need of extensive and long-term therapies. Occupational therapists will also be in demand at hospitals for both inpatient and outpatient services. Employment in schools is expected to increase as well.

Recently, OTs have been hired in more supervisory roles. With this in mind, future OTs can improve opportunities for advancement by taking appropriate management courses as electives during their undergraduate years. Additionally, you can advance in this field by specializing in a clinical area. Gerontology, mental health, and pediatrics are examples of these specializations. Finally, some OTs prefer to become faculty members and teach in accredited occupational therapy programs.

MEDICAL AND OSTEOPATHIC PHYSICIANS

Physicians and surgeons diagnose, prescribe, and administer treatment for individuals suffering from disease or injury. The two types of physicians recognized by the medical community are MDs (medical doctor or allopathic physicians) and DOs (doctor of osteopathic medicine). The two types of medical schools have similar curricula, with the first two years being classroom and laboratory oriented, while clinical rotations through the major medical specialties make up the third and fourth years. However, one difference in education between physician types is that students in osteopathic medicine begin learning touch and manipulation early in their medical education. Both types of medical education require residency training programs and an internship of various lengths, depending on the specialization chosen. Although both types of physicians use all accepted treatment methods, including pharmaceuticals and surgery, Doctors of Osteopathic Medicine emphasize the body's musculoskeletal system, preventive medicine, and a more holistic approach to patient care. Most MDs work in one or more specialties, including but not limited to anesthesiology, family and general medicine, internal medicine, pediatrics, obstetrics and gynecology, psychiatry, and surgery.

Where You Will Work

Internists, general and family practitioners, pediatricians, and other physicians work in private offices or clinics, with a small staff of nurses and other personnel. There is a trend to practice in groups, or health care organizations, in which group consultation on difficult cases can occur. Usually surgeons and anesthesiologists work in hospitals or surgical outpatient clinics. Most physicians and surgeons work long and irregular hours. In 2008, the Bureau of Labor Statistics reported that 43 percent of all physicians and surgeons worked in excess of 50 hours per week, whereas a small percentage (9 percent), worked part-time. Physicians and surgeons are on call, handling patient situations by phone, and making emergency visits to nursing homes, hospitals, rehabilitation centers, and clinics. Some physicians may choose to travel to disaster areas in the U.S. and around the world to work for various periods of time. Some have even given up their practice in the U.S. to provide services in impoverished third-world countries.

The Bureau of Labor Statistics reported that wages of physicians and surgeons are among the highest of any occupation, and vary by the type of practice. Wages varied across sources, but primary care physicians had a range for total median annual compensation reported between $157,250 and $186,044 (U.S.). Physicians who practiced in specialized medical fields reportedly earned a total median annual compensation of $339,738. Several factors affect wages, including the setting in which one works—hospital, clinic, or office—and the type of practice.

What You Will Do

All physicians obtain medical histories, perform examinations, and, on the basis of this information, order, perform, and interpret diagnostic tests. They also counsel patients on diet and nutrition, hygiene, and preventive health care. Physicians who specialize have more specific responsibilities. Anesthesiologists are primarily involved in the care of patients during surgery, and pain relief during and after surgery. These critical care specialists are responsible for maintaining the patient's vital life functions during surgery. They also work in the intensive care unit (ICU) and in labor and delivery, where they assist in alleviating pain. Family and general practitioners (i.e., the traditional family physician) are often the first line of defense for health care. These physicians typically have a set of regular patients for whom they assess and treat a wide range of illnesses, from the flu and sinusitis to setting broken bones and treating osteoporosis. These practitioners refer patients to specialists in cases of more serious conditions.

Internists specialize in the diagnosis and treatment of adults and see patients with a wide range of problems that affect internal organ systems, including the digestive and urinary systems. Internists rely on different techniques to treat patients, from use of pharmaceuticals to hospitalization. Again, if patients have more serious conditions, the internist will refer them to a specialist. In turn, patients from specialists often are referred to the internist. Other types of physicians include cardiologists, orthopedic specialists, radiologists, pathologists, allergists, and dermatologists.

Surgeons specialize in the treatment of injury, disease, and other conditions through the practice of surgery. Many surgeons specialize in a specific area, such as orthopedic surgery, neurosurgery, or cardiovascular surgery. Other types of surgeons include but are not limited to plastic surgeons, gastroenterologists, and ophthalmologists. Many surgeons perform several surgeries every day.

Whom You Will Work With

Physicians and surgeons work within a large arena of health care. They refer patients to other medical personnel depending on the diagnosis, and to physical and occupational therapists, as well as others, for treatment. They interact daily with patients and staff, including nurses, fellow physicians, clerical staff, and X-ray and laboratory technicians.

What Personal Skills and Abilities You Will Need to Succeed

The personal skills and abilities essential for success in the medical field are the same as those required for other health care careers. They include but are not limited to patience, active listening, critical thinking, reading comprehension, speaking and writing skills, time-management skills, judgment, decision-making skills, and monitoring skills. Physicians need very good personal and professional interaction skills because frequent interactions occur on both levels. Many conversations between doctors and patients require the utmost sensitivity and confidentiality. The physician must be able to communicate well both orally and in writing. Practicing medicine requires inductive and deductive reasoning, critical thinking, and problem-solving skills. It also requires a high degree of commitment to patients, self-motivation, and the ability to handle the pressures and long hours of medical education and practice. Physicians must be emotionally stable and able to make decisions in emergencies. They must be committed to ongoing study throughout their careers to learn about and apply medical advances.

What Education and Certifications You Will Need

Students interested in medical school should have undergraduate work in physiology, biology, physics, mathematics, and inorganic and organic chemistry, as well as in English, humanities, and the social sciences. Undergraduate kinesiology majors have a unique advantage over other undergraduate majors if they wish to pursue a career as a physician or surgeon because of the broad understanding this major provides regarding the functions and capabilities of the human body. Students should be involved in volunteer work at hospitals or clinics to gain practical experience in the profession.

Barbara J. Briner, DO

Private practitioner in osteopathic manipulative medicine and clinical professor at Michigan State University, College of Osteopathic Medicine

Briner points out that practicing medicine "takes genuine love for the work and for the patients. It takes dedication, listening, hearing, and caring. It takes curiosity and an ever new willingness to learn, to help, and to comfort."

Photo courtesy of Barbara Briner.

Most people would agree that formal education and training requirements for physicians are among the most demanding of any occupation; they include four years of undergraduate school, four years of medical school, and three to eight years of internship and residency, depending on the specialty. A few medical schools offer combined undergraduate and graduate (medical) school programs, which take six to seven years to complete. Most applicants to medical schools have a bachelor's degree, and some have graduate degrees. Acceptance to medical school is highly competitive. In addition to submitting transcripts, MCAT (Medical College Admission Test) scores, and letters of recommendation, schools are also concerned with the applicant's character, leadership abilities, and personality. They look for participation in extracurricular activities as well. Interviews are usually part of the acceptance procedure.

Classroom and laboratory experiences comprise most of the first two years of medical school. Students take such classes as anatomy, physiology, biochemistry, pharmacology, psychology, medical ethics, and laws governing medical practice. They learn to perform the intake skills necessary, such as medical histories, examination of patients, and diagnostic skills. The last two years are spent working under the supervision of physicians in clinics and hospitals, learning aspects of health care, including treatment of chronic and acute conditions and preventative and rehabilitative care. Students gain experience in diagnoses and treatments of illnesses during rotations through family practice, internal medicine, OB/GYN, pediatrics, psychiatry, and surgery.

Following medical school, MD students usually enter a hospital residency. The residency is in a specialty area and is paid, on-the-job training in medical education. Most DOs have a year-long internship after graduation from medical school, followed by a two- to six-year residency. A physician's training is extremely costly, with most medical school graduates incurring debt for educational expenses.

To practice medicine as a physician, all states, the District of Columbia, and U.S. territories require licensing. All MDs practicing in the United States must pass the United States Medical Licensing Examination (USMLE). Osteopathic physicians and surgeons must pass the Comprehensive Osteopathic Medical Licensing Exam (COMLEX). Graduation from an accredited medical school is a requirement to sit for either exam. Once licensed in one state, a physician usually can get a license to practice medicine in another state without further examination, although some states limit reciprocity. In general, graduates of foreign medical schools can qualify for licensure after passing an exam and completing a U.S. residency requirement. For further information on state licensure, contact that state's medical examining board. Board certification in a specialty might require spending up to seven years in residency training, depending on the specialty. A final examination must be taken immediately after residency, or after one or two years of practice.

Future Outlook

According to the Bureau of Labor Statistics, a 22 percent growth in employment of physicians and surgeons is expected between 2008 and 2018 owing to continued expansion of health care–related industries, and the need for replacing retiring physicians and surgeons. Additionally, the increasing geriatric and overall populations will drive the demand for physicians. The shortage of family practice and internist physicians has become a growing concern. How the rising costs of health care or new health care legislation will affect the job market remains unclear; what is clear is that disease and injury will continue to be part of our lives, and a trained medical force will always be needed to treat them.

CHIROPRACTOR

Chiropractors diagnose and treat patients with health problems of the musculoskeletal system that might have deleterious effects on the nervous system and on the patient's general health. Chiropractic is based on the theory that spinal joint misalignments interfere with the nervous system, resulting in a decreased resistance to disease and different conditions of diminished health. Doctors of chiropractic focus primarily on the patient's overall health, and alignment of the spine assists the body in its inherent recuperative abilities. According to the American Chiropractic Association, more than 22 million people visited a doctor of chiropractic in 2009.

Where You Will Work

Chiropractors work an average of 40 hours per week, often during evening hours and weekends to meet the needs of their patients. Similar to other health care practitioners, chiropractors in a group practice are sometimes on call, or they treat patients of other chiropractors in the group. A relatively small number of chiropractors teach, conduct research, or work in hospitals and clinics. Some allow other therapists to rent office space in their business, but typically they do not consult with these therapists. Practitioners of massage therapy and hypnotherapy are two examples of alternative therapists who might rent office space from chiropractors.

According to the Bureau of Labor Statistics, the median annual wage of salaried chiropractors was $66,490 (U.S.). The range for the middle 50 percent of wages earned was between $45,540 and $96,700 a year. As in all professions, geographic location, experience, and qualifications might influence earnings.

What You Will Do

Chiropractic physicians listen to patients' complaints, take their health histories, including results of physical, orthopedic, and neurological examinations, and order X-rays and other diagnostic images. These data allow the chiropractor to more closely examine the alignment of the spine. Posture and flexibility are analyzed not only through X-ray, but also by direct palpation of the spine and range-of-motion measurements. Leg length discrepancies are noted, and other physical alignments checked. Some chiropractors use procedures such as stretching, massage, heat, light, ultrasound, and acupuncture in their practices. Shoe inserts, bracing, tape and other supports might be recommended. Chiropractors counsel patients about health, including changes in lifestyle, exercise, nutrition, and stress management. Some specialize in areas such as sport injuries, orthopedics, pediatrics, diet and nutrition, and diagnostic imaging.

Whom You Will Work With

Chiropractors work independently or together with other chiropractors in a group practice. As such, they are also responsible for management of their business. Chiropractic patients are individuals who have (or have had) musculoskeletal injuries that might have affected their nervous system, or they are people who seek to avoid musculoskeletal imbalances and injuries and thus schedule regular appointments as preventive measures. Individuals of all ages and all activity levels seek chiropractic adjustments to keep themselves mobile and pain free without medication.

What Personal Skills and Abilities You Will Need to Succeed

The personal skills and abilities required for success in chiropractic are the same as those for other health practitioners. Critical thinking; listening; oral, reading, and written comprehension skills; time-management skills; speech clarity; good judgment; and the ability to solve problems are all important. Empathy, patience, compassion, and the drive to help others are essential qualities. Chiropractic requires exceptional observational skills to detect physical abnormalities. It takes manual dexterity, but not unusual strength to perform adjustments.

Linda A. Rassel

Doctor of chiropractic

Rassel has been in her own practice for over 30 years. She believes that "success in the practice of chiropractic health care requires a strong understanding of the *why* we do what we do, the *how* it allows for healing, and the *what* it means in our patients' lives. It requires a commitment to an idea greater than ourselves with a desire to serve our patients with unselfish love."

What Education and Certifications You Will Need

Chiropractors must have passed at least 90 credit hours of an undergraduate program, completed a four-year chiropractic program, and have passed both national and state examinations. The Council on Chiropractic Education (CCE) has accredited 16 chiropractic programs in the United States. Applicants must have undergraduate courses in English, organic and inorganic chemistry, physics, biology, psychology, and the social sciences or humanities. Undergraduate kinesiology majors are especially well prepared to study chiropractic because of the emphasis placed on understanding the human body's movements from a scientific perspective. Currently, a move is on to require a bachelor's degree for entry into accredited chiropractic schools. According to the Council on Chiropractic Education, schools of chiropractic require a minimum of 4,200 hours, with the first two years of classes devoted to theory and laboratory work, and the last two years focused on courses in manipulation, spinal adjustment, and clinical experiences in physical and laboratory diagnoses, neurology, orthopedics, geriatrics, physiotherapy, and nutrition. Upon graduation, chiropractic institutions and programs grant the degree of doctor of chiropractic (DC). Chiropractic schools offer postdoctoral training in many specialty areas, including sports injuries, rehabilitation, radiology, applied chiropractic sciences, and orthopedics. After completing their training, chiropractors may take examinations in their specialty from the corresponding chiropractic specialty board.

All states and the District of Columbia regulate the practice of chiropractic and grant licenses to those meeting the educational and examination requirements established by the respective state. Chiropractors can practice only in states in which they are licensed. Some states have reciprocal agreements that allow chiropractors to practice in another state without examination if they meet all of that state's requirements. Earning a license in most states requires passing a four-part exam given by the National Board of Chiropractic Examiners. Some states require an additional exam. To maintain licensure all states (except New Jersey) require completion of a specified number of hours of continuing education annually. Accredited chiropractic programs and chiropractic associations offer programs in continuing education.

Future Outlook

According to the Bureau of Labor Statistics, the demand for chiropractors is expected to increase 20 percent between 2008 and 2018, partially a response to the public's interest in alternative health care. Because chiropractic emphasizes the importance of healthy lifestyles, many health-conscious Americans find it appealing. The outlook for geriatrics and pediatrics chiropractic is especially bright because aging is usually accompanied by structural and mechanical problems, and the gentle nature of chiropractic treatment is attractive to children and their parents.

PHYSICIAN ASSISTANT

Physician assistants' (PAs) duties and responsibilities are somewhat akin to those of nurse practitioners, but they do not always have the authority to diagnose and manage illness as nurse practitioners do, because PAs practice only under the supervision of a physician or surgeon and as mandated by state law. Their training allows them to provide diagnostic, therapeutic, and preventive health care services as determined by a physician or surgeon and state law.

Where You Will Work

Most physician assistants work in primary care practices, such as family medicine, internal medicine, and pediatrics. With further training, the PA might be permitted to work in specialty areas such as general surgery, emergency medicine, orthopedics, and geriatrics. Those working in the surgical area provide pre- and postoperative care and might assist during surgery. PAs involved in surgery will stand for long periods of time. Work schedules vary according to the practice setting and depend on the supervising physician's hours. As is true for physicians, the PA's work in hospitals might include weekends, nights, or early morning hospital rounds, and they might be on call. PAs in clinics usually work about a 40-hour week. According to the Bureau of Labor Statistics, the median annual wage of PAs was $81,230 (U.S.) in 2008. The middle 50 percent range of PAs earned between $68,210 and $97,070. The lowest 10 percent earned under $51,360, and the highest 10 percent earned more than $110,240.

What You Will Do

As part of a health care team, physician assistants take medical histories; record intake and progress notes; examine and treat patients; order and interpret laboratory tests, and make diagnoses; instruct and counsel patients; and order and carry out therapy. Physician assistants may also prescribe certain medications. They give injections, suture wounds, order X-rays, and set fractures. Surgical PAs assist with most phases of surgery and medical complications. All diagnoses, therapy, and medical prescriptions performed by a PA are always reviewed by a supervising physician and are limited by state law.

In some cases, physician assistants have managerial responsibilities, such as placing medical supply and equipment orders, as well as supervising medical technicians and assistants. In some rural or inner-city population clinics, the physician might spend a limited amount of time at the clinic. In such cases, the PA provides the principle care for patients, and then discusses each case with the supervising physician and other medical professionals as required by law.

Whom You Will Work With

Physician assistants work shoulder to shoulder with supervising physicians and surgeons. They interact regularly with other health care professionals, including physical and occupational therapists, nurses, and nurse practitioners. PAs see patients with a variety of conditions and illnesses, as determined by the PA's certification and their supervising physician. If the supervising physician were a general practitioner or internist, the PA would see patients with a wide range of conditions, from childhood illnesses through elderly onset diabetes. If the PA were surgically certified, he or she would assist physicians during surgery or complicated medical procedures. The PA works with patients in the same manner as would their supervising physician.

What Personal Skills and Abilities You Will Need to Succeed

Personal skills and abilities required for PAs are similar to those of other positions in the health care profession; they include active listening, reading comprehension, and writing abilities. Speaking clearly and concisely and possessing good listening skills are essential to the position, as are critical thinking, judgment and decision making, monitoring skills, problem-solving abilities and the ability to engage in both inductive and deductive reasoning. Sensitivity to patient needs and needs of other health care personnel is important.

What Education and Certifications You Will Need

Requirements for admission to programs vary, but most require a college degree and health-related work experience. Usually an undergraduate program with a heavy emphasis on science is not required, but the scientific background mastered in a kinesiology program is excellent preparation for a physician assistant program. Full-time students can expect to spend at least two years in an accredited program. Many accredited PA programs have clinical teaching affiliations with medical schools. According to the Bureau of Labor Statistics, in 2008, 113 of 142 programs offered a master's degree, whereas other programs offered a variety of associate degrees, bachelor's degrees, and certificates. Many PA applicants have prior experience as health care professionals, such as athletic trainers, emergency medical technicians (EMTs), and paramedics.

PA education requires both laboratory and classroom coursework in anatomy, physiology, physical diagnosis, medical ethics, and clinical medicine. Supervised clinical training in family medicine, surgery, prenatal care and gynecology, geriatrics, emergency medicine, and other areas, is also required.

All states require physician assistants to complete an accredited educational program and pass a national examination to obtain a license. The National Commission on Certification of Physician Assistants (NCCPA) administers the Physician Assistant National Certifying Examination. This certifying exam is open only to graduates of accredited PA education programs. Passing the exam allows the PA to use the credential Physician Assistant–Certified. One hundred hours of continuing medical education must be completed every two years to remain certified. Every six years, the PA must either pass a recertification test or complete an alternative program that combines learning experiences with a take-home exam. Advancement for the PA requires additional education to specialize in an area such as internal medicine, emergency medicine, or pediatrics. This additional specialization is particularly useful when the PA is the primary medical person.

The Accreditation Review Commission on Education for the Physician Assistant (ARC-PA) requires all accredited physician assistants programs to offer graduate level degrees. The physician assistant bachelor's degree combines a bachelor's degree with a graduate level PA certificate; such programs usually admit students on a conditional basis until the first two years are completed. The physician assistant master's degree requires a bachelor's degree as a prerequisite for admission. The first year involves further coursework in classes such as anatomy and physiology, microbiology, internal medicine, obstetrics, gynecology, geriatrics, surgery, and psychology. Clinical experiences in primary care and medical specialties make up the second year.

Future Outlook

According to the Bureau of Labor Statistics, employment of PAs is expected to increase 39 percent from 2008 to 2018, significantly higher than for either physical therapists or occupational therapists. An increase in PAs is expected to provide greater accessibility of health care to the public and help cut health care costs. PAs will continue to relieve physicians of the more routine parts of the job, and their current range of responsibilities will likely increase as a result of these changes. Job openings are expected to rise in traditional and nontraditional medical settings, and especially in rural and inner-city clinics because of the difficulty of attracting and keeping physicians in those locations.

Jo Hartwell, RN, MS, head kinesiology advisor at Michigan State University was instrumental in providing information from which this chapter was developed. As always, Jo, many thanks.

Chapter 8

Careers in Higher Education

David I. Anderson

If a leisurely June, July, and August is your primary motivation for considering a job as a university professor, you better rethink your career plans. The idea that professors enjoy long holidays during breaks between semesters and have lots of free time is a myth. It is a myth perpetuated by people who have never spent much time in a university setting, let alone walked a day or two in a professor's shoes. Most professors are overworked and underpaid, particularly when you consider the length of time they spent in school to gain their academic qualifications. Nevertheless, working in higher education can be a highly rewarding and stimulating experience. You will experience the pride of a parent as you watch your students clear the academic hurdles associated with their programs of study. You will experience a different type of pride when you publish your first paper and consider the contribution you are making to knowledge. You might even be recognized for your contributions with awards or prizes. You will have opportunities to establish deep and lasting friendships with colleagues, to meet people from around the world, to visit different countries, to engage in lifelong learning, and to participate in stimulating exchanges of ideas. Moreover, you will have more control over what you do on a day-to-day basis than people in most other professions. However, don't be lulled into a false sense of expectation or get starry eyed. You will work incredibly hard to be an excellent professor—harder than people in many other professions.

University professors work within the education sector called postsecondary (after high school), or higher education. The higher education sector is comprised of many types of institutions and consequently many types of jobs, though all jobs share several features in common. What differentiates institutions is the degree of emphasis placed on particular tasks. Some institutions emphasize conducting research, and some place more emphasis on teaching. Others place equal emphasis on teaching, research, and service to the institution or the community. Regardless of the institution at which you work, you will need a minimum of a master's degree to gain entry into the profession. However, a doctoral degree (PhD or EdD) is the most common qualification held by people in higher education. Keep in mind that doctoral programs can take between four and six years to complete on top of a four-year bachelor's degree. You don't need to be the sharpest tool in the shed to complete a doctoral degree, but you must be one of the most resilient. Doctoral degrees test stamina and discipline as much as intellectual capacity.

This chapter provides details on the various kinds of institutions at which you might work and the types of jobs you might perform. You will learn about the many fields in which you can specialize, the people with whom you will work, the skills you need to succeed, the qualifications you require, and where to get them. You will also learn about the future outlook for academic careers. After completing the chapter you will be well positioned to determine whether an academic career is right for you.

Academia (or the *academy*) is a term used to describe the community of students and scholars engaged in higher education. More broadly, the term refers to the structures and mechanisms that create and transmit knowledge. The original Greek word, *Akademeia,* from which we get the current term, was a place on the outskirts of Athens. It was made famous by the Greek philosopher Plato, who acquired land there and established a place of teaching and learning.

Modern academia was shaped in the middle ages when Roman Catholic monasteries committed themselves to compiling a written record of the world's knowledge. Knowledge that had been preserved during the dark ages was disseminated in institutions that were the precursors to modern colleges and universities. Academia, as we know it today, is divided into disciplines or fields of study. These disciplines can be traced to the subjects that were taught in the middle ages, though they have been revised many times since then. The two major disciplines, the natural sciences and the social sciences, are divided and subdivided into the more specialized disciplines that are typically represented by individual departments or colleges in modern universities. However, professional training—as opposed to mastery of the knowledge within a specific discipline—is the focus of many departments and colleges. Professional training prepares the student for a particular career or profession, like medicine, law, or teaching. Many kinesiology programs are in professional colleges, such as a college of health and human services or a college of education. One of the most stimulating aspects of working in a department of kinesiology is that kinesiology draws on all of the major disciplines, and it also provides professional training. It is one of the few truly interdisciplinary, career-oriented fields of study!

WHERE YOU WILL WORK

Contemporary academic institutions come in many different shapes and sizes and are found all over the world. The basic classification system for American institutions of higher education is that established by the Carnegie Commission on Higher Education in 1970. The system has undergone many changes in recent years, but most people are familiar with the naming system that was in place prior to the current one. That system categorized institutions as either doctoral-granting institutions, comprehensive colleges, liberal arts colleges, two-year colleges and institutes, or professional schools and other specialized institutions. In the most recent classification system, institutions are divided into the following categories:

➤ **Associate's colleges** include institutions where all degrees are at the associate's level (i.e., degrees that usually take two years to complete) or where bachelor's degrees (degrees that take at least four years to complete) account for less than 10 percent of all undergraduate degrees.

➤ **Doctorate-granting universities** include institutions that award at least 20 doctoral degrees per year, not including degrees that qualify graduates for entry into professional careers such as doctor of medicine.

➤ **Master's colleges and universities** include institutions that award at least 50 master's degrees and fewer than 20 doctoral degrees per year.

➤ **Baccalaureate colleges** include institutions where baccalaureate (bachelor's) degrees represent at least 10 percent of all undergraduate degrees and that award fewer than 50 master's degrees or 20 doctoral degrees per year.

➤ **Special focus institutions** include institutions that award baccalaureate or higher-level degrees in which a high concentration of degrees is in a single field or set of related fields.

➤ **Tribal colleges** include colleges and universities that are members of the American Indian Higher Education Consortium.

The majority of kinesiology departments in the United States are housed in universities that *don't* grant doctoral degrees. A total of 63 universities in the United States offer doctoral programs in kinesiology. These programs are found in 35 states. Although more jobs are available at institutions that primarily offer baccalaureate and master's degrees as well as associate's degrees, many opportunities also exist to work at doctoral-granting universities. These positions are filled by people who have successfully completed a doctorate and show high potential for contributing to knowledge by conducting research. In many cases they will have published several articles by the time their doctoral studies are completed. In some cases they will have spent an extra year or two pursuing postdoctoral studies. But let's be clear on this: academics who do not work at doctoral-granting institutions also make important contributions to knowledge. Many professors seek out positions at baccalaureate institutions because they enjoy teaching and prefer to spend more time in the classroom than in the research laboratory.

Departments of kinesiology vary considerably in size. A small department at an associate's college might have fewer than half a dozen full-time faculty members. A large department at a doctoral-granting institution might have more than 20 full-time faculty members and possibly double that number in part-time faculty, who might be brought in to teach a class in a specialized area such as the activity program. Because kinesiology covers the theoretical and the practical study of physical activity, departments usually have a variety of part-time faculty who specialize in teaching a particular exercise or sporting activity, be it basketball, tennis, or soccer, or more contemporary offerings such as yoga, Pilates, or tai-chi. Sometimes coaches from the athletic department will teach in the activity program, and sometimes a full-time faculty member whose primary responsibilities are to teach theoretical courses and conduct research may also teach an activity class or two. However, with the financial pressures many departments are currently feeling, fewer full-time faculty members are teaching activity classes, particularly at baccalaureate, master's, and doctoral-granting universities.

Salaries vary depending on the type of institution, its geographic location, and level of appointment. Although actual salaries for professors can run well above $100,000 (U.S dollars) per year, the average salaries across all disciplines and institutional levels tend to be lower. Table 8.1 shows average salary levels at four-year institutions, as reported by *The Chronicle of Higher Education,* for the fields in which kinesiology programs are most often found.

Table 8.1   Average Faculty Salaries in U.S. Dollars by Field and Rank at Four-Year Colleges and Universities (2010–2011)*

	Professor	Associate professor	Assistant professor	New assistant professor	Instructor
Parks, recreation, leisure, and fitness studies	$80,703	$65,072	$54,039	$54,444	$43,503
Education	$83,748	$65,671	$55,848	$55,379	$46,183
Health professions and related clinical sciences	$95, 437	$75,207	$63,578	$64, 943	$52,720

*Data are for general categories of instructional programs in which kinesiology faculty typically reside.
Adapted from the Chronicle of Higher Education 2011. Available: http://chronicle.com/article/Chart-Average-Faculty/64500

Higher education is not a sector many people enter with an eye toward earning a great deal of money; that said, despite the long hours and modest salaries, there are many benefits to working in higher education. Here are just a few:

➤ Stability—while you might not make as much as some of your high-paid friends over any given five-year period, you will have a steady income. A steady income allows you to plan your life with a higher degree of certainty.

➤ Autonomy and flexibility—though you will work long hours, you decide when to do the work and have considerable control over what you do on a day-to-day basis. Moreover, you choose what topics to research, and you decide what content you will teach and how you will teach it, within reason.

➤ There is a clearly defined career progression with opportunities to pursue leadership or administrative positions, if they appeal to you.

➤ Health and retirement benefits—many universities offer good health and retirement or superannuation packages. When you add benefits to your take-home salary, your overall compensation can be considerably higher than it appears.

➤ Opportunity to make an important and enduring contribution to knowledge and be on the front line in the fight against some of society's most important challenges (e.g., the prevalence of obesity and cardiovascular disease).

➤ Opportunity to engage in lifelong learning and to be stimulated intellectually. The profession demands staying up to date with advances in your field of study.

➤ Opportunity to make a difference in the lives of young people and to teach, mentor, and shape the next generations of teachers and scientists.

➤ Opportunities for earning extra income through government and industry consulting and serving as an expert witness.

➤ Sabbaticals—every few years you have an opportunity to take a break and work somewhere else (often in another country) for a period of 6 to 12 months—one of the best perks in academia!

WHAT YOU WILL DO

Describing what professors do *not* do might be an easier task than describing what they do. A professor's job is multifaceted but usually includes most or all of the following tasks or duties: raising funds, publishing, teaching, mentoring, developing and maintaining collaborative relationships, networking, managing research projects, supervising research teams, attending conferences, writing papers, giving speeches, supervising graduate students, and engaging in administrative tasks. Many of the skills needed for success are learned through trial and error. The first few years are particularly tough because preparing new lectures is equivalent to writing several term papers each week, and this must be done while devoting time to committee work and establishing your reputation as a research scholar.

Three core responsibilities comprise the professor's job: teaching, research, and service. The emphasis each institution places on these responsibilities varies according to the mission of the institution, but the nature of the work is very similar regardless of where one works. At baccalaureate colleges and master's level colleges and universities, the emphasis tends to be spread about evenly: 33 percent teaching, 33 percent research, and 33 percent service. That said, in actuality professors at these institutions probably devote 60 to 80 percent of their work week to teaching, and the remainder is split between research and service. The split at a doctorate-granting university might be defined as 40 percent teaching, 40 percent research, and 20 percent service. But, really, professors might spend 50 to 60 percent of their work week engaged in research activities, 20 to 30 percent engaged in teaching, and the remainder in service. In addition, they likely will have the help of graduate students and sometimes postdoctoral fellows to assist them with teaching. Professors at doctorate-granting institutions are much more likely to teach small graduate seminars than large undergraduate lectures. However, such professors are under much more pressure to publish research papers, secure external funding for research, and establish a high profile in their field of study than are professors who work at baccalaureate institutions.

Teaching

Although disseminating knowledge is a core mission of institutions of higher education, most PhD programs do not prepare candidates to teach. Their primary focus is on ensuring each graduate has the requisite knowledge and skills to make a research contribution to the field of study. Generally that means the professor must master the broad knowledge base that underpins their field and develop a high degree of expertise in the knowledge, skills, and technologies associated with a specialized area in their field. Thus the early years of teaching can be quite frustrating as the professor decides what content to cover, develops a teaching style, and establishes which teaching methods work well and which should be discarded. Some universities offer teaching workshops as part of their professional-development program, but sometimes newly employed faculty find themselves too busy to attend them. Students will provide the major source of feedback on teaching effectiveness. The feedback comes at the end of the semester in the form of teaching evaluations. Importantly, universities use these evaluations as the primary source of evidence on which to base their own evaluation of a professor's teaching effectiveness.

Universities offer many types of classes, ranging from large lectures with several hundred students to more intimate seminars with fewer than 10 students. Seminars are highly cherished teaching assignments because they typically give professors an opportunity to explore an area of their expertise in depth with a group of motivated graduate students. Large lectures are more challenging. Student interest, motivation for studying the subject, and aptitude varies widely, and opportunities for asking questions and gauging student's understanding are limited. In large lectures the professor can feel more like a stage performer than a teacher.

Distance learning is becoming increasingly popular at many universities, and up-and-coming professors are advised to master the technologies and methods used in this highly expanding mode of teaching. Also, teaching methodologies employed in classrooms are becoming more and more linked to computer technology. Learning how to effectively employ the many instructional software packages on the market is now a must for the new professor.

Research

A passion for research is what attracts many academics to their careers. Research can stir all the emotions; making new discoveries is exhilarating if you're lucky enough to make them. However, the build-up to those discoveries can be filled with frustration. The nature of research varies from one subdiscipline in kinesiology to another. Qualitative methodology, in which people are observed in naturalistic settings or asked to report their feelings, beliefs, or attitudes on a topic, are used frequently by researchers interested in the sociocultural, philosophical, or historical bases of sport and physical activity and by those who conduct research on physical education pedagogy. In contrast, quantitative methods, which place a premium on measuring variables with great precision, are used more frequently by researchers interested in how physiological systems respond to exercise or how the laws of physics govern movements. Scientific understanding is advanced by both qualitative and quantitative methods, and researchers must be familiar with both methods, even if they prefer one over the other.

The setting in which research is conducted can also vary. Some researchers work in the field collecting data on athletes or on school children engaged in physical education, whereas others work in a laboratory. Some laboratory-based research is done on animals, and some is done on humans. Most laboratory researchers work with highly specialized equipment designed to yield highly reliable and accurate

Star Student: Nicole

Photo courtesy of Nicole Bolter.

While I thought I would be nervous showing up for my first day as a college professor, to my pleasant surprise, I was simply excited. This was because I realized that my training as a doctoral student had prepared me for the challenge. During graduate school, I was fortunate to teach my own undergraduate courses in my emphasis area (sport and exercise psychology) but also in broader areas in kinesiology (e.g., sociology of sport, history of sport). I gained hands-on teaching experience and valuable feedback from my advisor that helped me develop my own teaching strategies and philosophy. In addition, I learned in my doctoral program how to ask and answer important research questions about what interested me—positive youth development through sport. I was trained by my advisor and other graduate students through collaborative research but was also given the opportunity to develop my own research for my dissertation. I am thankful for these experiences because they taught me the skills I can use to pursue my own line of research and make a scholarly contribution to my field. In only my first year on the job, I am amazed how much my experiences in my doctoral program have helped me and am looking forward to further developing my skills as a teacher and researcher.

Nicole, College Professor (PhD in kinesiology)

measurements of what occurs during physical activity. Each subdiscipline has its own tools, which are used to measure activity in the brain, muscles, heart, or lungs, for example; analyze blood; or record reaction time, movement speed, coordination, or the forces that cause movement.

Reporting and disseminating research findings is an integral part of the research process. Researchers spend considerable time writing up their findings for publication and preparing presentations to deliver at scientific conferences. Publications that appear in prestigious journals are highly prized because they offer instant credibility and wide visibility. Generally, professor-researchers with higher public profiles are in higher demand and command higher salaries. Doctorate-granting institutions are very interested in securing high-profile researchers to enhance their reputations. The best paid and most prized positions in higher education tend to be reserved for the most productive researchers.

But research and teaching should not be viewed as independent responsibilities. Rather, they should be viewed as complementary. The most successful professors use their research interests to inspire their teaching and their teaching interests to inspire their research.

Service

Three types of service are important in a professor's job: service to the department and the university, service to the community, and service to the

Beverly Ulrich

Professor and director of the developmental neuromotor control laboratory at the University of Michigan

Professor Ulrich, who is internationally renowned for her research on motor control in typically and atypically developing children, has the following to say about the link between research and teaching: "One of the most exciting things about being a university professor is being able to combine your love of teaching with a passion for discovery. University professors conduct the science that propels our field to new and better practices that, in our role as teachers, we have the opportunity to share immediately with the future practitioners of that cutting edge knowledge."

Photo courtesy of Beverly D. Ulrich.

profession. Departmental and university service usually involve committee work or specialized tasks that contribute to the organization running smoothly. Universities vary in the emphasis they place on service to the community. More and more universities are looking to enhance their visibility in the local community because local community support can be vital to the success of many university initiatives. Of course, contribution to the local community is also central to the mission of higher education. Community service ranges from giving a presentation on one's area of expertise to a local group, to serving on community advisory boards, to setting up organizations to support community causes. Many kinesiology faculty members are engaged in community initiatives designed to promote physical activity. They might help police and fire departments develop fitness programs, and they often set up physical activity programs for school children. Some faculty use their expertise to consult with local businesses and government agencies.

Service to the profession usually involves assuming leadership positions in professional organizations, helping to organize conferences, reviewing manuscripts for professional journals, taking on editorial positions for journals, and reviewing grants for federal agencies. In addition, professors are regularly asked to write letters of recommendation for students applying to graduate programs, graduates seeking employment, or faculty members being considered for tenure or promotion. Writing letters of recommendation can consume a considerable amount of time.

Tenure

Tenure-track positions offer the possibility of earning guaranteed lifetime employment after successfully completing a probationary period that usually lasts six years. Tenure is the holy grail in academia. You will want to earn it because it is probably the best perk in the job! In a somewhat tongue-in-cheek review of Academia titled "What They Didn't Teach you in Graduate School: 199 Helpful Hints for Success in Your Academic Career," the authors Paul Gray and David Drew describe being a tenured full professor in a research university as the closest one can come to freedom in U.S. society. Though the merits of the tenure system have been debated for decades, and some have labeled the system antiquated and called for its abolishment, tenure is likely to be around for some time. The system was originally designed to promote and protect academic freedom—the freedom to say and do what you think is appropriate without bowing to outside political or financial pressures. (Because scientific progress relies on healthy debate and consideration of popular *and* unpopular positions, the entire academic enterprise could be compromised if academics were inhibited about expressing their beliefs.) Though tenure will likely survive, it is not clear how the number of tenure-track positions will be affected by the current budget crisis in higher education. Recent analyses have shown that the number of *non-tenure* hires has increased from a few percent in the 1970s to over 50 percent today. Most countries actually offer academic jobs as long term but limited contracts; the United States in an exception.

Faculty members typically enter their fields as assistant professors, progress to associate professors, and end their careers as full professors. The leap from assistant professor to associate professor usually comes after six years, when tenure is awarded. The time it takes to leap from associate to full professor depends on the institution. A particularly productive professor might get to this level in as few as three or four years, whereas others might spend their entire careers as associate professors.

Administrative Positions

Institutions of higher education are large bureaucracies; they consequently require large teams of administrators. Most administrators started as tenure-track faculty and moved into administrative positions after they were tenured. Most administrators don't start their careers with a view to becoming administrators. Usually professors become administrators after learning about university operations from the ground up. Such positions can be very rewarding, offering opportunities to learn new skills, shape the direction of the department or the university, and earn a higher salary. The administrative ladder typically has the following steps: department chair, assistant or associate dean, dean, provost or vice chancellor, president or chancellor. Kinesiology faculty members are often appointed to administrative or leadership positions within the university. Perhaps a lifetime of involvement with sport or physical activity provides the opportunities for developing the leadership skills, the organizational skills, and the discipline needed to be an effective leader or administrator.

WHOM YOU WILL WORK WITH

As you will appreciate from reading earlier chapters, kinesiology is a diverse field, including the study and teaching of physical activity and a range of theoretical subjects and professionally oriented courses. Despite the diversity, kinesiologists are united in their focus on physical activity. Each subspecialty approaches physical activity from a different perspective, though individual specialists are increasingly likely to participate on collaborative research projects. Many of the major issues tackled by kinesiologists, such as obesity and cardiovascular disease, are best handled by teams of researchers rather than individuals.

As academics and scholars, kinesiologists specialize in a focused area and usually establish professional relationships with others in that area—not merely across campus but across the country and the world. For example, exercise physiologists might collaborate with physiologists in the department of biology, biomechanists might collaborate with colleagues in engineering, and sport psychologists might work with colleagues in the department of psychology. Likewise, professors establish networks with academics at other campuses who are interested in studying the same problems. Entering a field of study is in many ways

Roberta Rikli

Former dean of the college of health and human development at California State University, Fullerton

Professor Rikli is internationally renowned for her research on health and well-being across the lifespan. She offers the following perspective on life as a college professor: "Being a college professor is one of the best jobs there is. You get to help teach and mentor enthusiastic young people who want to learn, you have flexibility in what you teach and when you teach, and you get to work with other faculty peers similar to yourself, as opposed to bosses or supervisors."

Photo courtesy of Roberta Rikli.

like entering a fraternity or sorority. A new knowledge base must be mastered, specific skills must be honed, a new (technical) language must be learned, and new relationships must be formed. Most fields of study, including kinesiology as a whole, are dominated by fewer than a hundred people. These are the power players who have built their reputations by consistently publishing in high-quality journals and getting grants or providing exceptional service to the profession. A few have established, or will establish, their reputations by writing textbooks that become popular in the field.

Students are the other people with whom you will frequently interact. They are your primary clients, after all. Like all people, students come in many varieties. The typical student is one who is motivated to get a degree, who shows up regularly to classes, who puts reasonable effort into assignments and exams, and who sees the value of a college degree. As you know, or soon will come to know, some students don't fit that mold. Some are lazy and happy to be left alone. Others are fiercely competitive and seek out professors at every opportunity. Some students are stubbornly independent. One of the most fascinating, and often frustrating, challenges of working with students is figuring out how to adapt to the smorgasbord of personalities that make up a class. Group dynamics magnify the challenge. What works well with one group of students can fail miserably with another. Graduate students present very different challenges from undergraduates, just as freshmen are different from seniors. You will certainly get a good sampling of the diversity of humanity during your career as an academic professor!

WHAT PERSONAL SKILLS AND ABILITIES YOU WILL NEED TO SUCCEED

An unbridled curiosity, a passion for learning, a thirst for new knowledge, and a very solid work ethic are four of the most important prerequisites for success in the field. Those traits must be balanced with patience, persistence, an ability to tolerate failure, and a willingness to learn from your mistakes. It is the nature of academic life to question ideas advanced by others and to have your own ideas scrutinized, questioned, and criticized as well. Consequently, a thick skin helps, as does a good sense of humor. An ability to relate to all types of people, an ability to adapt to change, an ability to multitask, and an ability to function without sleep are all important. In addition, a professor must be able to write well, speak confidently, and be fair, consistent, and diplomatic. Enjoying competition and cooperation is a great advantage. Mastery of the literature is essential, as is mastery of the scientific method and a number of specific research skills.

Of course mastery of teaching is also critical. However, as noted earlier, this important skill is usually learned on the job because most doctoral programs do not invest many resources in teaching students how to teach. Finding a good PhD

Richard Magill

Professor and chair of the department of teaching and learning in the Steinhardt School of Culture, Education, and Human Development at New York University

Photo courtesy of Richard Magill.

As a kinesiologist, Professor Magill has established himself as a leading authority in the area of motor control and learning. He offers this take on the qualities most likely to guarantee success as a university professor: "Success as a university professor demands a commitment to producing excellent scholarship, teaching, and service to your department, university, and profession. Included in this commitment should be a passion to acquire and disseminate new knowledge and to engage students in challenging learning experiences. In addition, a successful university professor has a work ethic that focuses on completing projects rather than attending to the hours worked. Finally, there needs to be a willingness to function as a cooperative and productive departmental citizen."

mentor is indispensable to ensure a smooth transition from graduate school to your first job. A good mentor is not necessarily the person with the biggest reputation in your field because the bigger the person's reputation, the less time they will have to spend with you. A good mentor is someone who knows the academic ropes, who is well regarded for teaching, research, and service, whose students historically have found good jobs, and who is willing to spend time honing your academic skills.

WHAT EDUCATION AND CERTIFICATIONS YOU WILL NEED

A PhD is the primary qualification you will need to work in academia. Although you can work at some community colleges and might be able to teach a class or two at a four-year college or university with a master's degree, tenure-track positions require a PhD. As noted earlier in the chapter, 63 universities in the United States currently offer doctoral degrees in kinesiology. Those departments that are members of the American Kinesiology Association are listed in figure 8.1. The National Academy of Kinesiology (NAK) conducts a five-year review and evaluation of doctoral programs in the United States (2001-2004 and 2005-2009). Although the review is limited to departments that volunteer to participate, the information can be of considerable help to students searching for doctoral programs. The rankings are available at the NAK website.

Completing an undergraduate degree in kinesiology is the most straightforward way to prepare for a PhD program. It is possible to gain entry into a PhD program in kinesiology with an undergraduate degree in another area, such as psychology or biology, however, sometimes students must spend time early in their program of studies taking undergraduate classes to make up for missing prerequisites. An undergraduate degree in kinesiology will provide all of the prerequisite classes the PhD program will look for on the transcript. Although at least a B+ average within the kinesiology major might gain you admission, most graduate committees will look for higher grades on subjects most relevant to the specialized area in which you plan to study. (For example, if you plan to study exercise physiology, the graduate admissions committee will look carefully to see how you performed in your undergraduate anatomy, physiology, chemistry, and exercise physiology classes.) It is wise to look at the entry requirements for the programs you might be interested in attending as early as possible in your undergraduate career so that you can plan your classes accordingly. You will also need to sit for the Graduate Record Examination (GRE) to gain entry into a PhD program. The scores required on the different sections of the examination vary from university to university.

Volunteering to work in an undergraduate department's research laboratories is an excellent way to determine whether a career as a professor in kinesiology might be right for you. Tenure track faculty are more than happy to take on undergraduate students as research assistants provided the students are motivated and willing to work hard and learn. Such experiences can help students determine which area(s) of kinesiology they find most interesting. Completing a master's degree en route to the PhD offers several advantages. First, it allows you to sample graduate school to see if you really want to spend four or five years there. Second, the PhD program will usually give you credit for the classes you took in the master's program, assuming those classes are relevant to the area in which you plan to study for your PhD. Third, you will gain valuable experience doing research, so you will have a better feel for whether research is something you want to spend a career doing. Fourth, you can prepare a better application for a PhD program by showing that you can handle graduate classes and by demonstrating a capacity to conduct independent research.

American Kinesiology Association Departments That Sponsor Doctoral Programs in Kinesiology

Arizona State University

Auburn University

Baylor University

Colorado State University

Florida State University

Iowa State University

Louisiana State University

Michigan State University

Middle Tennessee State University

Oregon State University

Penn State University

Purdue University

Springfield College (Springfield, MA)

Teachers College Columbia University

Temple University

Texas A&M University

University of Connecticut

University of Florida

University of Georgia

University of Houston

University of Idaho

University of Illinois at Urbana-Champaign

University of Maryland

University of Massachusetts

University of Miami

University of Michigan

University of Minnesota

University of New Mexico

University of North Carolina at Chapel Hill

University of North Carolina at Greensboro

University of Oklahoma

University of Texas at Austin

University of Virginia

University of Wisconsin

West Virginia University

Figure 8.1 The American Kinesiology Association consists of member departments from academic institutions from the United States and Canada. These academic departments cover a wide range of academic study and research related to the field of kinesiology.

Star Student: Tony

Photo courtesy of Anthony M. Mayo.

My interest in the field of kinesiology began after I completed my under- graduate degree. I enrolled at a master's university and took prerequisite courses to provide me with the foundation to succeed. I had the opportunity to interact with a diverse faculty from a variety of subdisciplines and to sample the core areas of kinesiology, which gave me a broader perspective on the discipline. This experience enabled me to determine my area of interest—motor learning and development. My mentors encouraged me to become active in research. My efforts ultimately led to publications and conference presentations. After completing the degree, I had the opportunity to teach undergraduate motor development and continue supporting faculty research efforts. I found that I am passionate about teaching college students and thrive in the dynamic research-oriented atmosphere afforded by the four-year university. This enthusiasm for teaching and research ultimately led to my decision to apply to a PhD program and fully embark on this challenging and rewarding career.

Tony, PhD student in motor learning and development

Finally, you'll have an opportunity to gain a different perspective on your field of study from that adopted by your PhD mentor.

Graduate school can be very stressful with its full load of classes, meetings with your advisor, and graduate assistantship duties. Nearly all PhD programs will offer teaching or research assistantships in which students might be asked to teach in the activity program (it really helps here if you have experience with a range of differ- ent sports and activities and if you specialize in one or two) or laboratory classes, grade papers, conduct literature searches, supervise undergraduate researchers, and collect data. The PhD student will not gain the experiences he or she needs to suc- ceed in an academic career by working a part-time job in an area outside of his or her major program of study. That said, you should accept your financial assistance with the full realization that many have described graduate student labor as the last form of legalized slavery in western society!

Graduate school can be a wonderful period of life. Your first day marks your formal entrance into the world of academia. You will meet fascinating people from all over the world, rub shoulders with great intellects, and establish friendships that will last a lifetime. You will be challenged and stimulated intellectually, you will travel to national and (if you're lucky) international conferences, and you will be exposed to a wide range of new ideas. You will look back on those days with fond memories!

FUTURE OUTLOOK

No matter what financial state the global economy faces, academics can be assured that they're engaged in a time-honored tradition that will likely be around, in some shape or form, for as long as civilization. Though many academics have seen their salaries stagnate (and in some cases go backward), particularly in those states that have been forced to furlough state workers to deal with mounting budget deficits, the demand for higher education remains strong. Demand typically increases during economic downturns as prospective employees see the benefits of staying in school. During tough economic times, academics are glad to be part of a tenure system.

A university degree makes a significant contribution to one's earning power. We are in the information age (the knowledge economy), and a competitive global market place for intellectual capital is pressing countries to enhance their innovative capacity. A person with a bachelor's degree earned almost twice that of a person with a high school diploma in 2007, according to U.S. Census Bureau data quoted by the American Association of University Professors. A master's degree raised income further by more than 20 percent, and a professional degree doubled the salary of a four-year college graduate. Governments and their constituents are becoming increasingly aware of the tremendous contribution that institutions of higher education make to the local and global economy. Jobs in higher education should become more abundant as a consequence. Whether those jobs will come with the same benefits as jobs in the past, such as opportunities for tenure, good health benefits, and retirement plans, remains to be seen. The beginning of the wave of retirements of senior faculty members in higher education is another factor to take into consideration. Pundits have been predicting a shortage of suitably qualified academics to fill the void for some years now.

Is the forecast for academics in kinesiology better or worse than in other fields of study? That's difficult to answer. However, a recent informal study of demand for degree programs in the California State University (CSU) system offers great promise for those considering kinesiology as an academic career choice. The study indicated that kinesiology was the fastest growing major in the entire university system. Many kinesiology programs on CSU campuses currently are struggling to meet the student demand. Many PhD graduates obtain academic appointments in the CSU system, and the student demand for access into kinesiology programs is high. We all hope this type of demand continues; there are potential boom times ahead for kinesiology. Anyone considering a career as an academic in kinesiology would do well to remember that a PhD opens doors to many different careers outside of higher education. Jobs exist in government, in industry, in the military, and in private foundations and nonprofit organizations. Thus, time spent pursuing a PhD and postdoctoral study does not need to be time wasted if the academic life ultimately does not appeal. The enterprising student can find many ways to put the advanced degree to good use.

Online Resources

Academy of Applied Personal Training Education
www.aapte.org

Accreditation Review Commission on Education for the Physician Assistants
www.arc-pa.org

American Academy of Physician Assistants Information Center
www.aapa.org

American Alliance for Health, Physical Education, Recreation and Dance
www.aahperd.org

American Association of University Professors
www.aaup.org/aaup

American Board of Medical Specialties
www.abms.org

American Chiropractic Association
www.acatoday.org/level1_css.cfm?T1ID=13

American College of Sports Medicine
www.acsm.org

American College of Surgeons
www.facs.org

American Council on Exercise
www.acefitness.org

American Kinesiology Association
www.americankinesiology.org

American Medical Association
www.ama-assn.org

American Occupational Therapy Association
www.aota.org/Consumers

American Osteopathic Association
www.osteopathic.org

American Physical Therapy Association
www.apta.org

American Society of Anesthesiologists
www.asahq.org/career/homepage.htm

Aquatic Therapy & Rehab Institute
www.atri.org

ASEP Professional Coaches Education Program
www.asep.com/about.cfm

Association for Applied Sport Psychology
http://appliedsportpsych.org

Association of American Medical Colleges
www.aamc.org/students

Bureau of Labor Statistics of the U.S. Department of Labor, "Occupational Employment and Wages, 2009-10 Edition"
www.bls.gov/oes/current/oes_stru.htm

Career Colleges
www.careercolleges.com/career-assessment-test.jsp

Career Explorer
www.careerexplorer.net/aptitude.asp

The Carnegie Foundation for the Advancement of Teaching
www.carnegiefoundation.org

Chronicle of Higher Education
http://chronicle.com/section/Home/5

Finding a Kinesiology Department That's Right for You

The **American Kinesiology Association (AKA)** is an association of over 100 college and university departments nationwide that prepare students for kinesiology careers. On its website, the **AKA** provides information regarding departments offering preparation in the career tracks discussed in this book. You can access this information at www.americankinesiology.org; click on the "Career Center" tab and then "Careers in Sport, Fitness, and Exercise." You will find instructions for identifying departments that sponsor curriculums matching your career interests.

Clinical Exercise Physiology Association
www.acsm-cepa.org

Commission on Dietetic Registration
www.cdrnet.org

Competencies for older adult exercise professionals
www.seniorfitness.org/National%20 Standards.htm

The Cooper Institute
www.cooperinstitute.org

Council on Chiropractic Education
www.cce-usa.org

Federation of Chiropractic Licensing Boards
www.fclb.org

Federation of State Medical Boards
www.fsmb.org

Gait and Clinical Analysis of Movement Society
www.gcmas.org

International Association for the Philosophy of Sport
http://iaps.net

International Fitness Professionals Association
www.ifpa-fitness.com

International Health, Racquet and Sportsclub Association
http://cms.ihrsa.org

International Society of Biomechanics in Sports
www.isbs.org

Job Diagnosis
www.jobdiagnosis.com/career-counseling.htm

LPGA Teaching and Club Professional Certification Program and Career Center
www.lpga.com/content_1. aspx?pid=2600&mid=13

National Academy of Kinesiology
www.nationalacademyofkinesiology.org

National Academy of Sports Medicine
www.nasm.org

National Association for Kinesiology and Physical Education in Higher Education
www.nakpehe.org

National Association for Sport and Physical Education
www.aahperd.org/naspe

National Athletic Trainers Association
www.nata.org

National Board of Chiropractic Examiners
www.nbce.org

National Commission on Certification of Physician Assistants, Inc.
www.nccpa.net

National Commission for Health Education Credentialing, Inc. (Certified Health Education Specialist)
www.nchec.org

National Council on Strength and Fitness
www.nscf.org

National Exercise and Sports Trainer Association
www.nestacertified.com

National Exercise Trainers Association
www.ndeita.com

National Federation of Professional Trainers
www.nfpt.com

National Federation of State High School Associations
www.nfhs.org

National Curriculum Standards to Prepare Senior Fitness Instructors
www.seniorfitness.net/National%20 Standards.htm

National Strength and Conditioning Association
www.nsca-lift.org

National Strength and Conditioning Association Certification
www.nsca-cc.org

The National Youth Sport Coaching Association
www.nays.org/coaches

North American Society for Sport History
www.nassh.org/NASSH_CMS/index.php

North American Society for Sport Management
www.nassm.com

North American Society for Sport Psychology and Physical Activity
www.naspspa.org

North American Society for the Sociology of Sport
www.nassh.org/NASSH_CMS/index.php

O*Net OnLine, "Summary Report for: 29-1065.00 - Pediatricians, General"

www.onetonline.org/link/ summary/29-1065.00.

O*Net OnLine, "Summary Report for: 29-1069.00 - Physicians and Surgeons, All Other"

www.onetonline.org/link/ summary/29-1069.00

O*Net OnLine, "Summary Report for: 29-1071.00 - Physician Assistants"

www.onetonline.org/link/ summary/29-1071.00

PayScale

www.payscale.com

PGA Education and Membership ("Steps to Becoming a PGA Member")

http://pgajobfinder.pgalinks.com/ helpwanted/empcenter/pgaandyou/pro. cfm?ctc=1637&CFID=1500770&CFTOK EN=21907690&jsessionid=8430c9953c2 22f59e29a1d433aa7d4194dfd

Referee magazine

www.referee.com

Silver Sneakers

www.SilverSneakers.com

Training and Wellness Certification Commission

www.acptcertification.com

Union of European Football Associations (UEFA)

www.uefa.com

U.S. Department of Labor (Bureau of Labor Statistics)

www.bls.gov

U.S. Soccer Federation

www.ussoccer.com

Index

Note: The italicized *f* and *t* following page numbers refer to figures and tables, respectively.

About the Editor

The **American Kinesiology Association** (AKA), an association of over 100 college and university departments, was formed in February 2007 by the Human Kinetics Foundation with the support of the National Academy of Kinesiology. The AKA promotes kinesiology as a unified field of study and serves as an advocate at academic, governmental, and professional levels, both nationally and internationally. The AKA serves the needs of kinesiology departments at colleges and universities, assists scholarly societies associated with kinesiology, and encourages cross-disciplinary study in kinesiology.

About the Contributors

David Anderson is a professor and former chair in the department of kinesiology at San Francisco State University and a longstanding member of the University of California's Institute of Human Development. His research on skill acquisition is widely cited and has attracted considerable media attention and external funding. He is committed to making an enduring contribution to knowledge in kinesiology in addition to helping students find their passion and reach their potential.

Wojtek Chodzko-Zajko is head of the department of kinesiology and community health at the University of Illinois at Urbana-Champaign. For the past 25 years his research has focused on the effect of exercise and physical activity on health and quality of life. Chodzko-Zajko is a member of the scientific advisory committee of the World Health Organization (charged with developing *WHO Guidelines for Physical Activity Among Older Persons*) and is chairman of the board of directors of the American Council on Exercise. He also served as founding editor of the *Journal of Aging and Physical Activity* from 1992 to 2002.

Marlene Dixon is an associate professor of sport management at the University of Texas at Austin. She is a research fellow in the North American Society for Sport Management and serves on the editorial boards of several leading sport management journals, including the *Journal of Sport Management* and *Sport Management Education Journal.* Her primary research interests are in the areas of sport and quality of life and improvement of the overall sport experience for participants.

Warren Franke is a professor in the department of kinesiology and director of the exercise clinic at Iowa State University. He has taught exercise programming courses at the college level for over 20 years. He has extensive experience developing exercise programs for a variety of participants ranging from cardiac and pulmonary rehabilitation patients to professional athletes. He also serves on the editorial board of *ACSM's Health & Fitness Journal.*

Kim C. Graber is an associate professor and associate head of undergraduate studies in the department of kinesiology and community health at the University of Illinois. She also is director of the college of applied health sciences teaching academy. She has served as president of the National Association for Sport and Physical Education, secretary of the Research Consortium, and chair of the Curriculum and Instruction Academy. Graber is a fellow of the research consortium of the American Alliance for Health, Physical Education, Recreation and Dance.

Rhonda Haag is currently a doctoral student in sport pedagogy at Purdue University. She has taught physical education and health since 1987 and has coached varsity-level track and field, basketball, and volleyball. She is an NCAA track and field All-American athlete and has served on the Oregon Physical Education Association board as secretary/treasurer and high school representative.

Jolene Henning has been a certified athletic trainer since 1996. She is an associate professor and director of the degree program for the master of science in athletic training at the University of North Carolina at Greensboro. She is a member of the National Athletic Trainers' Association professional education committee and chair of the clinical education subcommittee.

Shirl Hoffman is the AKA's former executive director and now editor of the e-magazine *Kinesiology Today*. He also is editor of the textbook *Introduction to Kinesiology, Third Edition* (2009, Human Kinetics), and is author of *Good Game: Christianity and the Culture of Sports* (2010, Baylor University Press). He is professor emeritus of kinesiology at the University of North Carolina at Greensboro, where he served as department head for 10 years.

Jamie O'Connor is a doctoral candidate in physical education pedagogy at the University of Illinois. She taught secondary physical education, health, and English for six years while simultaneously serving as assistant athletic director and coaching volleyball and basketball. She is studying middle school bullying in physical activity settings and recently received the Laura J. Huelster Award and the AIESEP Young Scholar Award.

Thomas Templin is a professor in the department of health and kinesiology at Purdue University. He has served as president of the National Association for Sport and Physical Education and chair of the Curriculum and Instruction Academy. He is a fellow of the Research Consortium of the American Alliance for Health, Physical Education, Recreation and Dance. He serves on the boards of the National Academy of Kinesiology, the American Kinesiology Association, and the International Association of Physical Education in Higher Education.

V. Dianne Ulibarri has research interests that include clinical gait analysis, injury mechanisms, and statistical approaches used in analysis of biomechanical data. She was editor for the *Basic Stuff Series I: Kinesiology, Second Edition* (AAH-PERD, 1987). Currently she an associate professor of kinesiology at Michigan State University, where she is also the kinesiology undergraduate coordinator, undergraduate study abroad coordinator, faculty advisor to Phi Epsilon Kappa, and KIN honors advisor.